Meals that Heal

Stop Start Eating and Grain Free Goodness

Diane Diaz and Sharon Howard

Table of Contents

Introduction

There's something wrong with the modern Western diet. Almost everyone agrees that the way we eat is responsible for a host of ailments, ranging from diabetes and heart disease to more subtle conditions like depression. Once intimately connected with nature, our food sources have become industrialized and more closely related to factories than farms. The result is an increase in all kinds of health problems, including unprecedented weight gain. It's simply too easy to eat badly.

If you find yourself frequently feeling tired, sick, out of sorts or otherwise physically unwell, it can be hard to figure out why. Doctors frequently ignore these symptoms, or tell you its all in your head. When they do acknowledge them, it's only to prescribe drugs that can be worse than the problem itself. Very rarely does the medical professional acknowledge that the issue could be in what you eat. For millions of people who suffer from food sensitivities, intolerances and allergies to modern products, however, a change in diet could be the ideal solution.

For some of us, the issue is wheat, modern versions of which seem designed to make you pack on the pounds. This is especially problematic for people who have digestive problems like celiac disease or intolerances for wheat proteins. Many other grains, including rye and barley, can cause the same issues. For other people, corn, rice or soy are the root of the problem. Unfortunately, these foods are in almost every product, making it difficult to find anything that doesn't induce symptoms.

Even the frequency with which you eat could be causing problems for your body. After all, humans didn't develop in situations where there was a lot of food available all the time. Your body might be putting on excess weight and developing issues because it expects to get less food than you're giving it. This might seem counter-intuitive, but it is a real problem. For a significant number of people, eating less occasionally can be the key to living a longer, happier, healthier life.

This book is divided into two main sections. The first focuses on grain-free diets to help people who suffer from health problems connected with these foods. The second shows you how to engage in intermittent fasting to better simulate the way the human body was designed to eat. Making either of these changes in your lifestyle can be very challenging, but it's a worthwhile endeavor for many people. After all, there's no benefit to feeling miserable, tired and overweight all the time when you could be much happier and healthier.

You'll find out all the ways in which grains, and particularly wheat, could be harming your health. For some people, it's the age of the grains that causes the problems. While wheat and other grains in their original forms might not be harmful, highly engineered modern wheat has been made to grow faster and be far more caloric than its ancestors. Its thinner germ means less fiber and fewer vitamins, making an entirely less nutritious and more harmful food.

This process has happened to more than just wheat. Over time, every grain that we eat has become industrialized. If you're someone who's sensitive to this kind of problem, you might be able to eat some older varieties of grains. Others will be unable to comfortably enjoy any grain at all. No matter which kind of grain intolerance you might suffer from, your health will improve if you switch from a normal, wheat-based diet to one that relies on other foods.

The recipes in this book are designed to help you do just that. You'll be able to enjoy grain-free foods for every meal, from baked omelets to grain-free coffee cakes for breakfast, savory black bean salad for lunch, and spicy meatballs for dinner. There are even delicious fries, cakes, chips and breads designed to help you win free of the dominance that wheat has in your diet. These meals will give you the ability to rest your system and heal your body. You'll feel better, stronger and happier.

You can combine the recipes you find in the portion of this book dedicated to grain free eating with the tips included in the second half. You can also use the recipes in that portion on their own. Either way, the information you find there will help you learn to eat less frequently and more mindfully.

The intermittent fasting process requires you to eat during specific times. This can either require you to eat one day and fast the next, or to fast for short periods of time during the day, then eat later. Both techniques help replicate the way we might have eaten before the advent of modern agriculture. After all, our ancestors couldn't necessarily rely on having a square meal three or more times per day. Their bodies were designed to take advantage of food whenever they had it, but in a modern context that leads to weight gain and poor health.

When combined with other healthy lifestyle choices, intermittent fasting can lead to a much better way of living. You just need to learn how to change your diet appropriately. The recipes in this book will help you do so. Consider having a breakfast of whole grain hot cereal with cherries or a Mexican breakfast casserole. Then fast throughout the day and finish in the evening with a hearty, nutritionally-balanced dinner. Italian chicken, vegetable pot pie or chicken tostadas will help you keep feeling great while you lose weight and rebalance your body.

No matter who you are, there's a good chance that modern life and the mechanized food production system are doing damage to your body. You don't have to put up with it, however. Finding the right meals that heal can do a lot to ensure that you get the nutrition you need, without the disruptive elements present in so many common foods. It's a great opportunity to get your health back under control!

Section 1: Grain Free Cookbook

Normally, when people talk about going grain free they mean particularly wheat free. Wheat is found in so many food products today, especially in processed foods. However, the there is a rise in the number of people who experience health issues if they consume wheat, and in particular, the gluten part of the wheat. With the rise of wheat or gluten intolerances and allergies, the need for more alternatives for food has surfaced. First, let's talk about the health issues consuming wheat may cause.

Health Issues From Consuming Wheat

Wheat has a high glycemic index level. This means it converts to "sugar" easily in the body, which in turns converts to excessive weight gain and fat. People wanting to lose weight may find if they avoid wheat, they lose the weight easier.

Allergies to wheat can cause symptoms of IBS or irritable bowel syndrome. Other issues that may show up are migraine headaches, asthma irritations, fatigue, skin issues, and yeast infections. Sometimes people will have one or more of these symptoms and after going off the wheat will find relief. If you have any of these symptoms, you may ask your healthcare provider about having an allergy test done to see if it is caused by wheat. Or try the diet and see if you have relief.

Autism patients may show improvement if they go on a gluten free diet. For parents of autistic children, this is good news, as it may provide some help in treatment. Again, ask the healthcare provider about this possibility.

Some people may have difficulties in the absorption of minerals if they consume wheat. This may be why they show the above symptoms. Certainly, it is best for the body if it is able to absorb all the nutrients from the foods we eat. Going on a grain free diet allows the body to have a chance to absorb all the nutrients from nutritious foods.

Tips for a Grain Free Diet

If you have studied the grain free diet you may have run across a diet called the Paleo Diet. This is a diet believed eaten by our Stone Age ancestors. The main component of the diet is the absence of grains. This grain free cookbook is not the Paleo Diet, because the recipes here do include foods on the "avoid" list for the Paleo Diet, but it is interesting that it is also a popular diet that works that does not include grains. Our Stone Age ancestors were a healthy bunch, living to ripe old ages (older than we do) and without many of the health ailments we suffer.

In addition to the recipes included in this book, there are ways to avoid grains if you stop and think about it. The first thing you should do is plan your meals. You may want to vary your meals, by cooking stuff that is not included in this book. That is okay, you stay "grain free" if you simply avoid grains. Here are some tips:

For breakfast, look at the recipes provided here and include healthy portions of eggs. Eggs are so versatile; you can fry them, scramble them, poach them, and boil them. And in addition to all of that, you can serve them with sautéed vegetables, cheese, or even with a slice of grain free bread or coffee cake. Eggs are a good source of protein and they give you a good energy boost to start your day.

Think outside the box of wheat products. If you love spaghetti, instead of reaching for the wheat laden noodles, grab a couple of zucchinis and slice them lengthwise into "noodles." Pour a bit of spaghetti sauce over and try the Herbed Parmesan Bread and you will have a delicious Italian meal. Carrots can be done this way as well.

Are you a pizza lover? Try making a flat omelet (there is those eggs again, versatile, aren't they?) and spread pizza sauce and toppings. You will not miss the wheat crust, because the flavors of the all the pizza will over power the egg. Try it you will be surprised!

If you do not have any bread ready for a sandwich, make a lettuce roll. Put all the items you would in your sandwich on a big lettuce leaf, roll it up and eat it. It will taste great and you will remain grain free. You can do the same thing with hamburgers, sloppy Joes, or any kind of sandwich meal.

Get to eating more soups and salads and forget sandwiches, if you are addicted to breads. Soups and salads are very satisfying and a lot more nutritious than 2 slices of wheat bread. Of course, if you are a hardcore sandwich lover, there is a recipe for wheat free sandwich bread in this book.

What About All the Hype About How It Is Healthy to Eat Whole Grains

It is true, if you research about going grain free you will find as many articles about how healthy whole grains are, and it can get confusing. The only way to know for sure if you have a gluten or wheat intolerance is either to have allergy tests performed, or try an elimination diet.

An elimination diet may be helpful in pinpointing whether or not certain foods actually cause issues or not. It takes a little while to figure this out though, you cannot just avoid a certain food for a day and figure it out. For one thing, it takes the body a couple of days to even a week or two for the side effects of certain foods to leave the body. With this in mind, if you do choose to try an elimination diet, you need to stick with it for at least three weeks to see the full effects.

If it is wheat foods that concern you and you wish to try the elimination diet to see if that indeed is the culprit to your health issues, this grain free cookbook is your perfect companion. Each recipe is completely wheat grain free, so you can easily plan three weeks' worth of meals to find out if wheat is your problem.

A Good Way to Get a Healthy Whole Grain

A food called quinoa acts as a grain, but in truth is even healthier than whole wheat. This food has been consumed for thousands of years. Quinoa is one of the "super foods" that packs a load of nutrition. What makes quinoa so wonderful is how it can be used in recipes. A few recipes within this book that contains quinoa and it is an excellent replacement for whole grains. The good thing about quinoa is that there are hardly any instances of people with "quinoa allergies" or "quinoa intolerances."

Suggestions for using this Grain Free Cookbook

The recipes within this book contain healthy whole ingredients. But the recipe by itself is not meant to be the only thing consumed. Include other foods with your meals. For example, eat salads with lunch and supper, steam vegetables for side dishes. Feel free to add to these recipes to enhance them. The recipes within this book may be similar to others, however each one is meant to be a part of the grain free diet and offers a variety in choices.

Grain Free Cookbook Recipes

Grain Free Breakfast Recipes

Vanilla Yogurt with Fruit Salad

A refreshing breakfast, and highly nutritious, you cannot go wrong with this delicious fruit salad with a sweet vanilla yogurt.

What You'll Need:

1 banana (just ripe, sliced)
1 bunch of seedless grapes (green, halved)
2 cups of yogurt (plain)
2 cups of strawberries (tops cut, halved)
1 cup of blueberries
1 cup of raspberries
2 tablespoons of honey
1 tablespoon of orange juice
1/2 teaspoon of vanilla extract

How to Make It:

Mix the 2 cups of plain yogurt with the 2 tablespoons of

honey and the 1/2 teaspoon of vanilla extract with a whisk. In a separate bowl, add the banana slices and the tablespoon of orange juice. Add the 2 cups of halved strawberries, cup of blueberries, cup of raspberries, and the bunch of seedless halved green grapes and toss with the banana slices. Divide the fruit into 6 individual bowls, top with the sweetened vanilla yogurt.

Makes 6 servings.

Oven Omelet

This is an easy omelet to make because you do not have to worry with flipping it in the pan. Just mix the ingredients and put in a baking dish and an hour later have a hot fresh omelet.

What You'll Need:

16 eggs
2 cups of milk
2 cups of cheddar cheese (sharp, shredded)
3/4 cup of turkey ham (cubed)
6 scallions (chopped)
salt and pepper

How to Make It:

Prep: Preheat the oven to 350 degrees Fahrenheit. Spray a 13x9 in baking dish with cooking spray.

Add the 16 eggs to a bowl and stir with a whisk, making sure to break each yolk. Pour in the 2 cups of milk and continue whisking. Add the 2 cups of shredded sharp cheddar cheese, 3/4 cup of cubed turkey ham, 6 chopped scallions, and season with salt and pepper. Stir to combine. Pour into the greased baking dish. Bake for about 47 minutes. Insert a knife in the middle, the omelet is cooked when the knife comes out clean. Allow to cool for ten minutes before serving.

Makes 12 servings.

Addition: Add 1/2 cup of finely chopped bell peppers to make it a western omelet.

Sweet Potato Breakfast Casserole

This is a different twist on a breakfast casserole with the addition of the sweet potato.

What You'll Need:

1 dozen eggs
1 pound of turkey breakfast sausage
2 1/2 cups of spinach (baby, chopped)
2 cups of sweet potatoes (diced)
1 scallion (diced)
salt and pepper
canola oil

How to Make It:

Prep: Preheat the oven to 375 degrees Fahrenheit. Spray a 9x13 inch baking dish with cooking spray.

First, add a little canola oil to a skillet and turn to medium high. Cook the pound of turkey breakfast sausage until browned. Add a little more canola oil if needed to cook the 2 cups of diced sweet potatoes until tender. Next, place the tender diced sweet potatoes in a large bowl. Toss in the 2 1/2 cups of chopped baby spinach, and the diced scallion. Add the cooked sausage

and the salt and pepper to taste to the vegetables.
Place into the greased baking dish. Next, crack the
dozen eggs in a large bowl and whisk until smooth. Salt
and pepper the eggs if desired. Pour the eggs over the
sausage and vegetables. Bake for about 27 minutes.
Remove from oven and sit for 10 minutes before cutting
and serving.

Makes 8 servings.

Nutty Hash

This chunky hash is full of the goodness of apples, squash and pecans and makes a hearty and satisfying breakfast.

What You'll Need:

2 cups of squash (butternut, diced)
1 1/2 cups of apples (tart, diced)
1/2 cup of pecans (chopped)
1/4 cup of scallions (chopped)
1/4 cup of onions (chopped)
2 tablespoons of olive oil
1/2 teaspoon of salt
1/2 teaspoon of black pepper

How to Make It:
Preheat the oven to low broil.

Heat a skillet on the stove on medium heat. Place the 2 cups of diced butternut squash onto a lined baking sheet. Broil and flip the squash every 3 minutes until it just starts to brown. Take out of the oven, turn oven off. Drizzle the 2 tablespoons of olive oil into the hot skillet. Add the 1/4 cup of chopped onions and sauté. Put the sautéed onions in a bowl. Add the 1/2 cup of chopped pecans to the skillet and heat through. Next add the 2 cups of browned squash, 1 1/2 cups of diced tart apples, the cooked onions to the heated pecans and stir a couple of times to combine, then allow to sit so it will soften. After a couple of minutes, flip and stir it to release the steam. Once browned to your liking, remove from heat. Sprinkle the 1/4 cup of chopped scallions over the top and sprinkle the 1/2 teaspoons of salt and pepper. Serve and enjoy.

Makes 4 servings.

Breakfast Burrito

Here is a delicious breakfast burrito made with turkey ham and the spiciness of salsa.

What You'll Need:

8 eggs
4 slices of ham (big enough slices to wrap with)
1/4 cup of spinach (chopped, baby)
1/4 cup of black olives (chopped)
1/4 cup of bell pepper (chopped, your color choice)
1/4 cup of tomato (chopped)
Salsa
Guacamole
Cilantro (for garnish)
Canola oil

How to Make It:

First, heat a skillet to medium high. Drizzle enough canola oil into a skillet to sauté the 1/4 cups of chopped baby spinach, black olives, bell pepper, and tomato. Whisk the 8 eggs in a bowl and pour over the cooking vegetable until scrambled. Even spoon the eggs onto each slice of turkey ham. Roll the turkey ham to make a meat burrito. Place back in the skillet, carefully rolling to heat and slightly brown the ham. Serve on a plate with salsa and guacamole. Garnish with a sprig of cilantro.

Makes 4 servings.

Apple Sausage

This is actually a very different sausage, pork-free and made with chicken and apples.

What You'll Need:

1 pound of ground chicken
1 large apple (peeled, cored, grated)
1 egg
1 teaspoon of salt
1/2 teaspoon of basil (dried)
1/2 teaspoon of cumin (ground)
1/2 teaspoon of marjoram (dried)
1/2 teaspoon of oregano (dried)
1/2 teaspoon of sage (dried)
1/2 teaspoon of thyme (dried)
1/4 teaspoon of black pepper

How to Make It:

Prep: Preheat the oven to 350 degrees Fahrenheit. Line a baking sheet with parchment.

Beat the egg first, then add it to the 1 pound of ground chicken, 1 large apple (peeled, cored, grated), 1 teaspoon of salt, 1/2 teaspoon of basil (dried), 1/2 teaspoon of cumin (ground), 1/2 teaspoon of marjoram (dried), 1/2 teaspoon of oregano (dried), 1/2 teaspoon of sage (dried), 1/2 teaspoon of thyme (dried), and 1/4 teaspoon of black pepper. With hands, mix the ingredients. Form into 18 patties and place on the baking sheets, sides not touching. Bake for 10 minutes and flip, then bake another 10 minutes.

Makes 9 two-patty servings.

Coffee Cake

There is nothing more mouthwatering than the smell of delicious coffee cake baking first thing in the morning.

What You'll Need:

4 eggs
1 cup of pecans (chopped)
3/4 cup of arrowroot flour
3/4 cup of coconut flour (sifted plus 1 teaspoon)
1/2 cup of almond milk
1/2 cup of honey (plus 2 tablespoons)
1/2 cup of butter (1/4 cup melted and 1/4 cup softened)
2 teaspoons of baking powder
1 1/2 teaspoons of cinnamon (ground)
1/2 teaspoon of salt

How to Make It:

Prep: Preheat oven to 350 degrees Fahrenheit. Spray an 8x8 inch baking pan with cooking spray.

In a bowl, beat the 4 eggs then combine with the 1/2 cup of almond milk, 1/2 cup of honey, and the 1/4 cup of melted butter. In a separate bowl, combine the 3/4 cup of arrowroot flour, 3/4 cup of sifted coconut flour, 2 teaspoons of baking powder, and the 1/2 teaspoon of salt. Gradually add the dry ingredients into the batter, stirring to combine.

In another separate bowl, make the streusel. Combine the 1 cup of chopped pecans, 1/4 cup of softened butter, 2 tablespoons of honey, and the 1 1/2 teaspoons of ground cinnamon.

Pour half of the batter into the greased baking dish. Sprinkle half of the streusel. Pour the remaining batter over the streusel and sprinkle the remaining streusel on top. Bake until a knife inserted in the middle comes out clean, about half an hour.

Makes 6 to 8 servings.

Grain Free Snacks, Appetizers, and Desserts

Peanut Butter Cookies

A very chewy and delicious peanut butter cookie, you will enjoy eating.

What You'll Need:

2 cups of peanut butter
2 cups of sugar (granulated, plus extra for dusting)
2 eggs (slightly beaten)
2 teaspoons of vanilla extract
Coarse salt granules

How to Make It:

Prep: Preheat the oven to 350 degrees Fahrenheit.

Combine the 2 cups of peanut butter, 2 cups of granulated sugar, 2 beaten eggs, and the 2 teaspoons of vanilla in a bowl. Drop by the tablespoonful's onto a baking sheet (ungreased), and flatten crisscross with a fork. Sprinkle extra sugar and coarse salt granules over the top. Bake for about ten minutes until the cooked turn a golden brown. Keep an eye, oven baking times vary. Let sit in baking sheet for 2 minutes before carefully removing with a spatula to a wire rack for continued cooling.

Makes 3 dozen.

Cajun Fries

This is a nutritious snack but tastes like it's forbidden because of its wonderful spiciness. Enjoy!

What You'll Need:

10 carrots (peeled, cut into thin sticks)
1 tablespoon of olive oil
1/4 teaspoon of cayenne pepper (OR use a Cajun seasoning)
Salt and Pepper
Dipping sauce

How to Make It:

Prep: Preheat the oven to 450 degrees Fahrenheit. Spray a baking sheet with cooking spray.

Put the carrot sticks in a large zipper bag and drizzle the tablespoon of olive oil, 1/4 teaspoon of cayenne pepper and some salt and pepper into the bag. Zip and shake to coat each carrot stick. Next, place the carrot sticks onto the baking sheet and place in the oven for about 15 minutes. Turn each "fry" over and continue to bake for another 15 minutes. Delicious served warm.

Dipping sauce: Try your favorite dipping sauce for French fries or chicken strips. For example, ranch dressing, honey mustard, or ketchup.

Curry Pumpkin Seeds

For those who love curry seasoning and pumpkin seeds you will love this snack!

What You'll Need:

2 cups of pumpkin seeds
2 egg whites
4 teaspoons of curry powder
salt

How to Make It:

Prep: Preheat the oven to 375 degrees Fahrenheit. Place a piece of foil over a baking sheet.

Whisk the 2 egg whites together with the 4 teaspoons of curry powder and as much salt as you'd like. Place the 2 cups of pumpkin seeds into a large bowl with a lid. Pour the seasoned egg whites over the pumpkin seeds, place the lid on the bowl and shake, to evenly coat all the pumpkin seeds. Spread out over the foil in a single layer on the baking sheet. Bake until the seeds turn a golden brown, about 12 minutes. You can store in a zipper back and sprinkle more curry powder and salt as desired.

Oatmeal Chocolate Chip Raisin Cookies

These cookies are chewy, spicy, and perfect for a snack or treat.

What You'll Need:

4 1/2 cups of oats (old fashioned)
1 cup of butter (softened)
3/4 cup of sugar (granulated)
3/4 cup of chocolate chips (your favorite kind)
3/4 cup of raisins
1/2 cup of brown sugar (light, packed)
2 eggs
2 tablespoons of cornstarch
2 teaspoons of vanilla extract
1 1/2 teaspoons of cinnamon (ground)
1 teaspoon of baking powder
1/2 teaspoon of salt

How to Make It:

Prep: Preheat the oven to 350 degrees Fahrenheit. Line a cookie sheet with parchment.

Add 1 1/2 cups of the old fashioned oats to a food processor or blender and process to a fine meal. Stir in the 2 tablespoons of cornstarch, teaspoon of baking powder, and the 1/2 teaspoon of salt.

In a separate bowl, combine the cup of softened butter with the 3/4 cup of granulated sugar and the 1/2 cup of packed light brown sugar. Use an electric beater to mix for about a minute. Add the 2 eggs and the 2 teaspoons of vanilla extract and beat for another minute. Turn the beater to low and gradually add the prepared 1 1/2 cup of oats, for about a minute. Scrap the beaters. Fold in the remaining 3 cups of oats, 3/4 cup of chocolate chips, and the 3/4 cup of raisins.

Drop a large heaping tablespoon of dough onto the lined cookie sheet, leaving a 2 inch space between the cookies. Bake for about 15 minutes, until golden brown. Let the cookies cool for two minutes before carefully removing to a wire rack.

Makes 3 dozen cookies.

Classic No Bake Cookies

This is a classic favorite, like a candy bar in the shape of
a cookie!

What You'll Need:

3 cups of oats (quick cooking)
2 cups of sugar (granulated)
1/2 cup of peanut butter
1/2 cup of butter
1/2 cup of milk
3 tablespoons of cocoa powder (unsweetened)
1 teaspoon of vanilla extract
pinch of salt

How to Make It:

Place a saucepan on high heat and add the 2 cups of
granulated sugar, 1/2 cup of butter, 1/2 cup of milk, and
the 3 tablespoons of unsweetened cocoa powder. Stir
continually until the mixture boils and boil while stirring
for 60 seconds. Turn the heat off but keep on the
burner. Add the 3 cups of quick cooking oats, 1/2 cup of
peanut butter, and the teaspoon of vanilla extract,
stirring until the peanut butter melts and all combines.
Drop by spoonful's onto waxed paper to form into
cookies and cool. Store uneaten portions in the

refrigerator.

Makes 4 dozen.

Banana Date Cookies

This delicious snack is as nutritious as it is tasty.

What You'll Need:

3 bananas (ripe)
2 cups of oats (rolled)
1 cup of dates (pitted, chopped)
1/3 cup of canola oil
1 teaspoon of vanilla extract

How to Make It:

Prep: Preheat the oven to 350 degrees Fahrenheit.

First, peel the bananas and mash them in a bowl. Add
the 2 cups of rolled oats, 1 cup of pitted and chopped
dates, 1/3 cup of canola oil, and the 1 teaspoon of
vanilla extract. Mix and set aside for 15 minutes. Drop
by spoonful's onto an ungreased baking sheet. Bake
until light golden brown, about 20 minutes. Cool before
serving.

Makes 3 dozen.

Ginger Cookies

These are like ginger snaps only they have coconut and cinnamon.

What You'll Need:

2 cups of almond flour
1/2 cup of coconut (grated)
1/3 cup of honey
4 tablespoons of butter (melted)
1 teaspoon of ginger (ground)
1/2 teaspoon of cinnamon (ground)
1/4 teaspoon of baking soda
1/8 teaspoon of salt

How to Make It:

Prep: Preheat oven to 300 degrees Fahrenheit. Spray a cookie sheet with butter flavored cooking spray.

In a bowl, add the 1/2 cup of coconut , 1/3 cup of honey, 4 tablespoons of butter,
1 teaspoon of ginger, and 1/2 teaspoon of cinnamon and combine by stirring. In a separate bowl combine the 2 cups of almond flour with the 1/4 teaspoon of baking soda and 1/8 teaspoon of salt. Stir the dry ingredients

into the batter. Shape into palm sized balls (about an inch in diameter) and place on the greased cookie sheet. Bake until golden brown for about 12 minutes.

Makes 2 to 3 dozen cookies (depending on how big you make them).

Raisin Spice Nut Cake

A delicious spice cake chocked full of walnuts and raisins.

What You'll Need:

2 1/2 cups of almond flour

2 eggs (beaten)

1/2 cup of yogurt (plain)

1/2 cup of walnuts (chopped)

1/3 cup of raisins

1/3 cup of honey

4 tablespoons of butter (melted)

1 teaspoon of vanilla extract

1 teaspoon of cinnamon (ground)

1 teaspoon of allspice

1/2 teaspoon of nutmeg (ground)

1/2 teaspoon of baking soda

1/4 teaspoon of salt

1/4 teaspoon of cloves (ground)

How to Make It:

Prep: Preheat the oven to 300 degrees Fahrenheit. Spray an 8x8 inch baking pan with cooking spray. Combine the 2 beaten eggs with the 1/2 cup of plain yogurt, 1/3 cup of honey, 4 tablespoons of melted butter, and the teaspoon of vanilla extract. In a separate bowl, combine the 2 1/2 cups of almond flour with the teaspoons of ground cinnamon, allspice, 1/2 teaspoons of ground nutmeg, baking soda, 1/4 teaspoons of salt and ground cloves. Gradually add the dry ingredients into the batter. Fold in the 1/2 cup of chopped walnuts and the 1/3 cup of raisins.   Pour the batter into the prepared 8x8 inch baking pan and bake until the top is golden brown, about half an hour.

Makes 6 to 8 servings.

Tortilla Chips

These "tortilla" chips can go either salty or sweet, whichever your tastes happens to be when you make them.

What You'll Need:

8 egg whites
1/2 cup of water
1/4 cup of coconut flour (raw)
1/4 teaspoon of baking powder
Butter
(salt OR cinnamon and sugar)

How to Make It:

Combine the 1/4 cup of raw coconut flour with the 1/4 teaspoon of baking powder. Add the 8 egg whites and the 1/2 cup of water using a whisk until all lumps are gone. Heat a skillet with some butter. Pour 1/4 of the batter into the hot buttered skillet (as if you are making crepes or pancakes, it does not take long so keep an eye on it). Allow the tortilla to "fry," when the edges are starting to brown, flip the tortilla, and cook for an additional 30 seconds. Do this for 4 tortillas.
Once done, let it cool a minute, then break them up into

"chips." Either salt them or sprinkle with cinnamon and sugar.

Makes 4 servings.

Grain Free Breads

Irish Soda Bread

This is a classic bread, enjoyed as a treat on St. Patrick's Day, but can also be enjoyed anytime as a grain free bread.

What You'll Need:

1 1/2 cups of rice flour (white)
1 cup of buttermilk
1/2 cup of tapioca flour
1/2 cup of sugar (granulated)
1 egg
1 teaspoon of baking soda
1 teaspoon of baking powder
1 teaspoon of salt

How to Make It:

Prep: Preheat the oven to 350 degrees Fahrenheit. Spray a 9 inch round pan with cooking spray.

In a bowl, combine the 1 1/2 cups of white rice flour, 1/2 cup of tapioca flour, 1/2 cup of granulated sugar, with the teaspoons of baking soda, baking powder, and salt. In a separate bowl, combine the cup of buttermilk and egg with a whisk. Pour into the center of the dry ingredients and stir until moistened. Batter may be lumpy. Pour into the prepared pan and bake for a little over an hour. Cake is done when a toothpick inserted in the middle comes out clean. Cool for 10 minutes, set pan on 2 knives or on a wire rack. Remove from pan and store wrapped in foil or plastic. Bread is best if it sits for a day before serving.

Makes 6 to 8 servings.

Corn Bread

Bake a pan of cornbread to go with a pot of beans or a bowl of chili.

What You'll Need:

2 eggs (lightly beaten)
1 1/2 cups of water (room temperature)
1 1/2 cup of cornmeal (fine)
1 cup of millet flour
1 cup of rice flour
1/4 cup of sugar (granulated)
1/4 cup of canola oil
1 tablespoon of baking powder
1 teaspoon of salt

How to Make It:

Prep: Preheat the oven to 350 degrees Fahrenheit. Spray a 9x9 inch baking pan with cooking spray.

In a bowl, combine the 2 lightly beaten eggs with the 1 1/2 cups of room temperature water and the 1/4 cup of canola oil with a whisk. In a separate bowl, combine the 1 1/2 cups of fine cornmeal, 1 cup of millet flour, 1 cup of rice flour, 1/4 cup of granulated sugar, tablespoon of baking powder, and the teaspoon of salt. Pour the liquid into the center of the dry ingredients and stir until just moistened. It may be slightly lumpy. Pour into the prepared 9x9 inch baking dish and bake for about 20 minutes, until the top turns golden and springy.

Makes 12 servings.

Herbed Parmesan Bread

This delicious herbed bread goes well with steamed vegetables and meat dishes.

What You'll Need:

2 1/2 cups of almond flour

1 cup of Parmesan cheese (grated)

3/4 cup of cottage cheese (large curd)

1/2 cup of water

2 eggs

3 tablespoons of butter (melted)

1 teaspoon of garlic (minced)

1/2 teaspoon of basil (dried)

1/2 teaspoon of baking soda

1/2 teaspoon of salt

1/3 teaspoon of oregano (dried)

1/3 teaspoon of thyme (dried)

How to Make It:

Prep: Preheat the oven to 325 degrees Fahrenheit. Spray 2 regular sized loaf pans with cooking spray.

Combine the 2 1/2 cups of almond flour with the cup of grated Parmesan cheese, 1/2 teaspoons of dried basil, baking soda, salt, 1/3 teaspoons of dried oregano, and dried thyme. Place the 3/4 cup of large curd cottage cheese, 1/2 cup of water, 2 eggs, 3 tablespoons of melted butter, and teaspoon of minced garlic into a food processor or blender. Blend until smooth. Add to the dry ingredients bowl and combine with a spoon. Divide the dough into 2 and place into the 2 loaf pans. Bake for just under an hour, when the top is golden brown.

Makes 2 loaves.

Banana Bread

This could be in the dessert section too, because it is that good.

What You'll Need:

3 cups of almond flour
1 cup of walnuts (chopped fine)
1/4 cup of honey
2 eggs (beaten)
2 bananas (ripe, peeled, mashed)
3 tablespoons of butter (melted)
3/4 teaspoon of baking soda
1/4 teaspoon of salt

How to Make It:

Prep: Preheat oven to 300 degrees Fahrenheit. Spray 2 regular sized loaf pans.

In a bowl, combine the 1/4 cup of honey, 2 beaten eggs, 2 ripe, peeled and mashed bananas, and 3 tablespoons of melted butter. In a separate bowl, combine the 3 cups of almond flour with the 3/4 teaspoon of baking soda, and 1/4 teaspoon of salt. Add the dry ingredients to the batter and mix. Stir in the cup of fine chopped

walnuts. Divide equally between the two loaf pans.
Bake for 50 minutes. Cool completely before serving.

Makes 2 loaves.

Sandwich Bread

This bread is perfect for making sandwiches or toast.

What You'll Need:

1 cup of cashew butter (room temperature)
4 eggs (separate the whites from the yolks)
1/4 cup of almond milk
1/4 cup of coconut flour
1 tablespoon of honey
2 1/2 teaspoons of apple cider vinegar
1 teaspoon of baking soda
1/2 teaspoon of salt

How to Make It:

Prep: Preheat oven to 300 degrees Fahrenheit. Place a sheet of parchment paper at the bottom of an 8.5x4.5 inch loaf pan. (Glass pan works best) Lightly spray the sides with cooking spray.

In a bowl, use an electric mixer to combine the cup of room temperature cashew butter with 4 egg yolks. Mix in the 1/4 cups of almond milk, tablespoon of honey, and the 2 1/2 teaspoons of apple cider vinegar for about a minute. In a separate bowl, add the 4 egg whites and beat them until stiff peaks form. In yet another bowl, combine the 1/4 cup of coconut flour with the teaspoon of baking soda and 1/2 teaspoon of salt. Next, add the dry ingredients to the milk mixture and beat for about a minute. Add the egg whites and beat long enough until it mixes well.   Add the dough to the prepared loaf pan and bake until a toothpick inserted in the middle comes out clean for around 47 minutes, until the top turns a nice golden brown. Immediately loosen the sides with a knife and remove loaf from pan and place on a wire rack for cooling before it is served.

Makes around 12 servings.

Zucchini Bread

This delicious zucchini bread is very moist and completely wheat free.

What You'll Need:

1 1/2 cups of zucchini (mashed)
1 1/2 cups of almonds (ground)
3/4 cup of almond butter
1/4 cup of arrowroot flour
1 egg
5 tablespoons of maple syrup
2 tablespoons of coconut oil
1 1/2 teaspoons of cinnamon (ground)
1 teaspoon of nutmeg (ground)
1 teaspoon of vanilla extract
1 teaspoon of baking soda

How to Make It:

Preheat oven to 325 degrees Fahrenheit. Lightly spray a regular sized loaf pan with cooking spray.

In a bowl, combine the 1 1/2 cups of mashed zucchini, 3/4 cups of almond butter, egg, 5 tablespoons of maple syrup, 2 tablespoons of coconut oil, and the teaspoon of vanilla extract. In a separate bowl, combine the 1/4 cup of arrowroot flour with the 1 1/2 teaspoon of ground cinnamon, teaspoon of ground nutmeg, and the teaspoon of baking soda. Add the dry ingredients to the wet ingredients, mix well. Add the 1 1/2 cups of ground almonds. Pour into the prepared loaf pan. Bake for 50 minutes. Allow to cool before serving.

Makes 1 loaf of bread.

Grain Free Side Dish Recipes

Broccoli Quinoa Casserole

This is the perfect side dish to pair with chicken or beef.

What You'll Need:

1 bunch of broccoli (florets, chopped)
1 tomato (chopped)
1 1/3 cups of water
1 cup of quinoa
1 cup of celery (chopped)
1/2 cup of onion (chopped)
3 tablespoons of soy sauce
2 tablespoons of brown rice vinegar
1 tablespoon of sesame oil (hot pepper)
2 teaspoons of curry powder
1/2 teaspoon of garlic (minced)

How to Make It:

Prep: Preheat the oven to 350 degrees Fahrenheit.

Place a skillet on medium high heat. Add the cup of quinoa and stir until it turns a golden brown and pops.

Add the quinoa to a regular sized casserole dish. Pour in the 1 1/3 cups of water. Place a large pot on the stove and turn to medium high. Drizzle the hot pepper sesame oil into the pan, then sauté the 1/2 cup of chopped onions, 2 teaspoons of curry powder with the 1/2 teaspoon of minced garlic. Combine in the pot with the chopped broccoli florets, chopped tomato, and the cup of chopped celery. Stir and cook for 3 minutes. Add the3 tablespoons of soy sauce and the 2 tablespoons of brown rice vinegar. Stir to combine and heat through. Pour over the quinoa. Bake in the oven until the top starts to brown, about 45 minutes. Let sit for 10 minutes, then serve.

Makes 4 servings.

Savory Black Bean Salad

This delicious salad has the savory and spicy flavor of the southwest with delicious couscous and black beans.

What You'll Need:

8 scallions (chopped)
2 cans of black beans (drained, 15 oz. each)
1 1/4 cups of chicken broth
1 cup of couscous (uncooked)
1 cup of corn (frozen, then thawed)
1/2 cup of bell pepper (red, seeded and chopped)
1/4 cup of cilantro (fresh, chopped)
3 tablespoons of olive oil (extra virgin)
2 tablespoons of lime juice
1 teaspoon of apple cider vinegar
1/2 teaspoon of cumin (ground)
salt and pepper

How to Make It:

Pour the 1 1/4 cups of chicken broth into a large saucepan and turn heat to high to bring to a boil. Add the cup of uncooked couscous and place a lid on the saucepan. Turn off heat and move pan off the burner for 5 minutes. Using a whisk, combine the 3 tablespoons of extra virgin olive oil, 2 tablespoons of lime juice, teaspoon of apple cider vinegar, with the 1/2 teaspoon of ground cumin in a bowl. Toss in the 8 chopped scallions, 2 cans of drained black beans, cup of thawed corn, 1/2 cup of chopped red bell pepper, and the 1/4 cup of fresh chopped cilantro. Next, using a fork, fluff the couscous and toss into the vegetables. Add salt and pepper to taste. Serve and enjoy.

Makes 8 servings.

Shrimp Soup

This soup makes a great lunch or a filling supper.

What You'll Need:

3/4 pound of shrimp (fresh, peeled, deveined)
3 cups of vegetable juice
1 bottle of clam juice (8 oz.)
1/2 cup of water
1/2 cup of long-grain white rice (uncooked)
1/2 cup of bell pepper (green, chopped)
1/4 cup of scallions (sliced)
1 bay leaf
1 tablespoon of butter
1/2 teaspoon of garlic (minced)
1/2 teaspoon of salt
1/4 teaspoon of thyme (dried)
1/4 teaspoon of basil (dried)
1/4 teaspoon of red pepper flakes
hot pepper sauce

How to Make It:

Place a large saucepan on stove and turn to medium heat. Add the tablespoon of butter and when it melts, add the 1/2 cup of chopped green bell pepper, 1/4 cup of sliced scallions, and the 1/2 teaspoon of minced garlic and sauté. Add the 3 cups of vegetable juice, bottle of clam juice, and the 1/2 cup of water and stir. Sprinkle in the 1/2 teaspoon of salt, 1/4 teaspoons of dried thyme, basil, and red pepper flakes. Add the bay leaf. Add the uncooked 1/2 cup of long-grain white rice. Turn to high until it boils, then turn to low to simmer, with cover, for 15 minutes, or until the rice is tender. Add the shrimp and cook for an additional 5 minutes. Remove and discard the bay leaf. Season with dashes of hot pepper sauce.

Makes 4 servings.

Mushroom Broccoli Tofu Quinoa

This is a hearty side dish but can double as a main dish because it is packed full of protein. It is perfect for vegetarians.

What You'll Need:

1 1/4 cups of vegetable broth (divided)
1 cup of spinach (chopped fresh)
1/2 cup of quinoa (uncooked)
1/2 cup of broccoli florets
1/2 cup of tofu (firm diced)
1/4 cup of mushrooms (sliced)
2 teaspoons of olive oil
2 teaspoons of garlic (minced)

How to Make It:

Pour the cup of vegetable broth into a saucepan and turn stove to high to bring to a boil. Add the 1/2 cup of uncooked quinoa, stir, reduce heat to low, cover with a lid and simmer for 20 minutes. Meanwhile, drizzle the 2 teaspoons of olive oil in a skillet and turn heat to medium. Add the 1/2 cup of broccoli florets, 1/2 cup of firm diced tofu, and the 2 teaspoons of mince garlic. Combine and then cover, turn heat to low and let sit for

2 minutes while it steams. Add the cup of chopped fresh spinach, 1/4 cup of vegetable broth, and the 1/4 cup of sliced mushrooms and stir. Turn heat up to medium, cover and cook for three more minutes. Add the vegetables to the quinoa pot, stir, cover, and sit with stove off for another 10 minutes. Transfer to a serving bowl, serve, and enjoy.

Makes 4 servings.

California Black Beans

This is a nice side dish that tastes great cool or warm.

What You'll Need:

4 cups of salsa

2 avocados (cubed)

1 1/2 cups of corn (whole kernels)

1 can of black beans (drained, rinsed)

1 cup of water

1/2 cup of quinoa

How to Make It:

Pour the water into a saucepan and add the 1/2 cup of quinoa. Turn the stove to high to bring to a boil. Turn heat to medium low while quinoa cooks, until the water is absorbed, may take about 10 to 15 minutes. Pour the 1 1/2 cups of whole kernel corn and the can of drained, rinsed black beans into a serving bowl, toss in the cooked quinoa. Served with generous portion of salsa and cubed avocados on top.

Makes 4 servings.

Stuffing

This is the perfect side dish to go with any meat, or even a vegetable meal.

What You'll Need:

1 pound of sage turkey sausage
2 turnips (peeled and cubed)
1 apple (peeled, cored, diced)
5 cups of button mushrooms (diced)
3 1/2 cups of sweet potatoes (peeled and cubed)
2 1/2 cups of celery (diced)
1 1/2 cups of onions (diced)
2 1/2 teaspoons of garlic (powder)
2 1/2 teaspoons of sage (powder)
2 teaspoons of salt
1 teaspoon of oregano (dried)
1 teaspoon of rosemary (dried)
1 teaspoons of thyme (dried)
1 teaspoon of turmeric
1 teaspoon of black pepper
Canola oil (for cooking)

How to Make It:

Prep: Preheat the oven to 375 degrees Fahrenheit.

Spray 2 baking sheets with cooking spray.

Place the 2 peeled and cubed turnips and the 3 1/2 cups of peeled and cubed sweet potatoes in a large bowl. Spray the turnips and sweet potatoes with cooking spray. In a small cup add the 2 1/2 teaspoons of garlic powder, 2 1/2 teaspoons of sage powder, 2 teaspoons of salt, 1 teaspoon of dried oregano,1 teaspoon of dried rosemary, 1 teaspoons of dried thyme, 1 teaspoon of turmeric, and the 1 teaspoon of black pepper and combine.   Sprinkle the seasonings over the sweet potatoes and turnips and toss to evenly coat. Spread the turnips and sweet potatoes out on the 2 baking sheets and place in the oven for an hour, turning every 15 minutes.

Meanwhile, add a little canola oil and cook the turkey sage sausage in a skillet until well done and brown. Add more canola oil if necessary, toss in the 2 1/2 cups of diced celery and the 1 1/2 cups of diced onions and sauté. Add the 5 cups of diced button mushrooms and the peeled, cored and diced apple, cook until they soften. Sprinkle extra seasonings over the sausage mixture if desired. Combine with the turnips and sweet potatoes. Spray a large baking dish - or a large roasting pan with cooking spray. Pour the contents into the pan. Reduce oven temperature to 350 degrees Fahrenheit and cook for half an hour. Alternatively, refrigerate the stuffing up to a day before cooking and serving.

Makes 8 servings.

Kale Mango Salad

A delicious and refreshing side dish.

What You'll Need:

1 bunch of kale (remove stalks, coarsely chopped)
1 cup of mango (diced)
1/4 cup of olive oil (plus a drizzle, extra virgin)
2 1/4 tablespoons of pumpkin seeds (toasted)
2 tablespoons of lemon juice (divided)
2 teaspoons of honey
Salt and pepper

How to Make It:

First, place the coarsely chopped kale in a large bowl, add a tablespoon of lemon juice and a drizzle of extra virgin olive oil. With hands, work the salt and lemon juice into the leaves, about 2 1/2 minutes of rubbing. Set to the side. In a separate smaller bowl, combine the remaining tablespoon of lemon juice with the 2 teaspoons of honey and several shakes of pepper. Add the 1/4 cup of extra virgin olive oil and continue whisking until it is well combined. Place the kale in 4 salad plates; divide the dice mango and pumpkin seeds. Drizzle the dressing over the salad and enjoy.

Makes 4 servings.

Grain Free Main Dish Recipes

Parmesan Mushrooms Quinoa

This dish is simply too hearty to be a side dish, it is a very tasty Italian style dish.

What You'll Need:

1 package of button mushrooms (8 ounces, chopped)
3 cups of chicken broth
1 1/2 cups of quinoa (rinsed)
1/2 cup of onions (chopped)
1/3 cup of Parmesan cheese (grated)
1 tablespoon of olive oil
1 tablespoon of butter
1/2 teaspoon of garlic (minced)

How to Make It:

Drizzle the tablespoon of olive oil into a skillet and turn heat to medium. Add the package of chopped mushrooms, 1/2 cup of chopped onions, and the 1/2 teaspoon of minced garlic and cook for five minutes, until well browned. Remove from heat. Add the tablespoon of butter to a saucepan and turn heat to medium high. Pour in the 1 1/2 cups of rinsed quinoa and brown, a couple of minutes. Add the 3 cups of chicken broth and turn to high until it boils, then reduce to simmer, for about ten minutes. Add the sautéed mushrooms, garlic, and onions and stir for 2 more minutes. Serve with Parmesan cheese sprinkled on top.

Makes 6 servings.

Meaty Red Beans and Rice

This dish is so good and the leftovers are even better.

What You'll Need:

1 pound of ground beef (lean)
1/2 pound of turkey kielbasa sausage (cut into bite sized chunks)
1 can of kidney beans (drained)
1 cup of pinto beans (canned, rinsed)
1 cup of vegetarian baked beans
3 1/4 cups of rice (white, uncooked)
1/4 cup of onion (minced)
1/2 teaspoon of cayenne pepper (ground)
canola oil

How to Make It:

Cook the 3 1/4 cups of rice according to package directions. Pour a little canola oil in a skillet and heat to medium high. Cook the 1/2 pound of turkey kielbasa sausage for about 7 minutes, stirring often to lightly brown on all sides. Sprinkle the 1/2 teaspoon of ground cayenne pepper. Put the turkey kielbasa sausage into the pot of rice. Add a little extra canola oil to the skillet if necessary, turn to medium high heat, and cook the pound of lean ground beef until browned. Add the pot of rice and sausage, add the 1/4 cup of minced onion, and continue to cook for another five minutes. Add the can of drained kidney beans, cup of caned, rinsed pinto beans and the cup of vegetarian baked beans, turn to simmer to heat through, stirring often. Add water if necessary to keep from sticking. Ready to serve when hot.

Makes 8 servings.

Fried Rice

This is a delicious main dish, hearty and filling, goes well with steamed vegetables or a salad.

What You'll Need:

1 package of green peas (frozen, 10 oz.)
1/2 pound of ground beef (lean)
2 scallions (chopped)
1 1/3 cups of rice (white, uncooked)
1 2/3 cups of water
1/8 cup of soy sauce
3 eggs (lightly beaten)
3 teaspoons of canola oil (divided)
1/4 teaspoon of salt
1/8 teaspoon of black pepper

How to Make It:

Add the 1 2/3 cups of water to a sauce pan and turn on high to bring to a boil. Add the 1 1/3 cups of white uncooked rice. Reduce the heat to low, stir, and cover. Simmer for 20 minutes. Crack the 3 eggs into a bowl and lightly beat. Add the 1/4 teaspoon of salt and 1/8 teaspoon of black pepper. Drizzle 1 teaspoon of canola oil in a large skillet and heat to medium high. Add the eggs, allowing them to cook evenly, stirring. Put in a bowl and set to the side. Cook the 1/2 pound of lean ground beef in the skillet until well browned. Drain the grease and put into another bowl.   Drizzle the remaining 2 teaspoons of canola oil into the skillet and add the cooked rice. Stir the rice to fluff it. Add the cooked ground beef along with the cooked eggs, chopped scallions, and the 1/8 cup of soy sauce. Heat through, several minutes and serve hot.

Makes 4 servings.

Jambalaya

If you love the spiciness of Cajun food, you will love this Jambalaya dish.

What You'll Need:

2 chicken breasts (boneless, skinless, cut into bite sized chunks)
1/2 pound of turkey kielbasa sausage (diced)
4 cups of chicken stock
2 cups of rice (white uncooked)
1/2 cup of onion (diced)
1/2 cup of bell pepper (green, diced)
1/2 cup of celery (diced)
3 bay leaves
2 tablespoons of garlic (chopped)
2 teaspoons of Worcestershire sauce
2 teaspoons of olive oil
1 teaspoon of hot pepper sauce
1/2 teaspoon of onion powder
1/4 teaspoon of cayenne pepper
salt and pepper

How to Make It:

Drizzle the 2 teaspoons of olive oil in a large pot and

turn stove to medium high heat. Add the chunked chicken breasts and diced turkey kielbasa sausage and cook until done, several minutes. Add the 1/2 cup of diced onion, 1/2 cup of diced green bell pepper, 1/2 cup of diced celery, and the 2 tablespoons of chopped garlic and sauté for another five minutes. Add the 1/2 teaspoon of onion powder, 1/4 teaspoon of cayenne pepper, and dashes of salt and pepper and stir. Pour in the 2 cups of white uncooked rice and the 4 cups of chicken stock and stir. Add the 3 bay leaves and turn the heat to high to bring to a boil. Cover, reduce heat to simmer until the rice is tender, for about 20 minutes. Add the 2 teaspoons of Worcestershire sauce and the teaspoon of hot pepper sauce, toss and serve.

Makes 6 servings.

Stuffed Cabbage

This is a wonderfully filling delicious meal, the stick to your ribs kind.

What You'll Need:

1 pound of ground beef (lean)
1 head of cabbage
1 can of tomato juice (12 oz.)
1 cup of rice (cooked)
1 egg
1 tablespoon of vinegar
1 tablespoons of sugar (granulated)
garlic powder
water

How to Make It:
Rinse head of cabbage, peel off first outer layer of leaves and place into a large pot, add water to cover and place on stove on high heat to bring to a boil. Continue to boil until the cabbage is soft, about 15 minutes. Carefully remove the core, leaving the leaves intact. Next, in a bowl, add the pout of lean ground beef and mix together with the cup of cooked rice, egg, and a couple of dashes of garlic powder. Mix with your hands, forming balls that fit in your hand. Pull a leaf from the

cabbage and roll around the ball of meat, completely encasing the meat. Continue to do this until all the meat is gone. Place any leftover cabbage leaves in the bottom of a large pot. Place the cabbage rolls onto the leaves. Pour in the can of tomato juice, tablespoon of vinegar, tablespoon of granulated sugar, and add just enough water to cover the top of the cabbage rolls. Turn heat to medium low, cover the pot, and let simmer for an hour. Do not let the leaves burn.

Makes 8 servings.

Spicy Meatballs and Rice

This is a great main dish for beef lovers, with a Mexican twist.

What You'll Need:

1 pound of ground beef
1 can of tomato puree (14.25 oz.)
1 can of Mexican-style corn (11 oz., drained)
2 cups of water
1 cup of rice
1 cup of onions (minced and divided)
1 bay leaf
2 tablespoons of white vinegar
1 tablespoon of canola oil
2 tablespoons of parsley (dried divided)
1 tablespoon of brown sugar
2 1/2 teaspoons of oregano (dried, divided)
1 1/2 teaspoons of cumin
1 teaspoon of garlic (minced)
1/2 teaspoon of chili powder
salt and pepper

How to Make It:

In a bowl, add the pound of ground beef with the

tablespoon of dried parsley, 1 1/2 teaspoons of dried oregano, and salt to taste. Add the 2 cups of water to a saucepan and pour in the cup of rice. Turn heat to high to bring to a boil. Cover, reduce heat to simmer and cook for 20 minutes. Meanwhile, add the tablespoon of canola oil to a skillet and turn heat to medium. Add 1/2 cup of minced onions and 1/2 teaspoon of minced garlic and sauté. Add onions and garlic to the ground beef mixture. With hands, form two dozen meatballs. Add the meatballs to the already hot skillet, and brown all over. Next, drain most of the fat from the skillet. Leave enough to add the remaining 1/2 cup of minced onions and 1/2 teaspoon of minced garlic, and sauté this. Add the can of tomato puree, tablespoon of dried parsley, tablespoon of brown sugar, 1 teaspoon of dried oregano, 1 1/2 teaspoons of cumin, 1/2 teaspoon of chili powder, and salt and pepper, and stir. Add the bay leaf. Cook for about 20 minutes, until the liquid thickens. Continue to stir and add the meatballs, cooking an additional ten minutes. Make sure the meatballs are completely cooked. Stir in the can of Mexican-style corn and heat through. Serve over a bed of cooked rice.

Makes 4 servings.

Stuffed Peppers

A delicious main dish filled with seasoned beef.

What You'll Need:

6 bell peppers (green, cut the tops off and carefully
remove the stem and seeds)
1 pound of ground beef (lean)
2 cans of tomato sauce (8 oz. each)
1 cup of water
1/2 cup of rice (white, long grain, uncooked)
1 tablespoon of Worcestershire sauce
1 teaspoon of Italian seasoning
1/4 teaspoon of garlic powder
1/4 teaspoon of onion powder
salt and pepper

How to Make It:

Prep: Preheat the oven to 350 degrees Fahrenheit.

Pour the cup of water into a saucepan, add the 1/2 cup
of uncooked long grain white rice, and turn the heat to
high. Bring to a boil, cover, reduce the heat to low and
simmer for 20 minutes. Add the pound of lean ground
beef to a skillet and cook on medium until brown. Next,

place the 6 prepped green bell peppers in a baking dish, openings on top. In a bowl, add the cooked ground beef along with the cooked rice, 1 8 oz. can of tomato sauce, tablespoon of Worcestershire sauce, 1/4 teaspoon of garlic powder, 1/4 teaspoon of onion powder and salt and pepper. Divide and spoon into each green bell pepper. In a separate bowl, mix the remaining 8 oz. can of tomato sauce with the tablespoon of Italian seasoning. Drizzle the sauce over the tops of the green bell peppers. Bake for an hour, basting with the tomato sauce at least 4 times.

Makes 6 servings.

Salmon and Rice

This is a delicious and nutritious meal made with smoked salmon and tasty fried rice.

What You'll Need:

6 cups of water
3 cups of rice (uncooked, long grain, white)
4 oz. of smoked salmon (chopped)
2 eggs (beaten)
1 scallion (chopped)
3 tablespoons of canola oil (divided)
1/2 cup of English peas (frozen)
1/4 cup of onions (fine chopped)
salt and pepper

How to Make It:

Add the 6 cups of water to a large saucepan on the stove on high heat. Add the 3 cups of uncooked long grain white rice and bring to a boil. Cover, reduce heat to low, and simmer until the rice is tender, about 20 minutes. Next, pour 2 tablespoons of canola oil into a skillet on medium heat. Add the 2 beaten eggs and scramble. Place eggs in a small bowl and set aside. Add the remaining tablespoon of canola oil to the skillet keep heat on medium. Add the chopped scallion and the 1/4 cup of fine chopped onions and sauté. Add the 4 oz. of chopped smoked salmon, cooked rice, scrambled eggs, and the 1/2 cup of frozen English peas and combine well. Season with salt, pepper, and heat through.

Makes 6 servings.

Seafood Gumbo

A hearty meal of seafood gumbo tastes great and is very filling if served over a bed of rice.

What You'll Need:

1 pound of shrimp (peeled, deveined, shelled)

7 cups of vegetable stock

2 cups of celery (chopped)

2 cups of onion (chopped)

2 cups of oysters (shucked)

2 cups of bell pepper (chopped, 1 red and 1 green)

1 1/2 cups of tomato sauce

1 cup of crabmeat

3/4 cup of canola oil

1 bay leaf

3 tablespoons of cornstarch

2 teaspoons of hot pepper sauce

1 1/2 teaspoons of paprika

1 teaspoon of garlic (minced)

1 teaspoon of salt

1/2 teaspoon of thyme (dried)

1/2 teaspoon of oregano (dried)

1/2 teaspoon of cayenne pepper (ground)

1/2 teaspoon of white pepper (ground)

1/2 teaspoon of black pepper (ground)

How to Make It:

In a small cup, combine the 1 1/2 teaspoons of paprika, teaspoon of salt, 1/2 teaspoons of dried, thyme, dried oregano, ground cayenne pepper, ground white pepper, and ground black pepper. Add the bay leaf. Set aside. Place a heavy large pot over medium high heat; add the 3/4 cup of canola oil. Stir in the 2 cups of chopped celery, 2 cups of chopped onion, 2 cups of chopped red and green bell peppers. Turn the heat to high, stirring often, add the 3 tablespoons of cornstarch, 2 teaspoons of hot pepper sauce, teaspoon of minced garlic, and the small cup of herbs, and stir for 5 minutes. Add the 1 1/2 cups of tomato sauce and keep stirring while turning the heat to high. Pour in the 7 cups of vegetable stock and bring to a boil. Turn heat to low and simmer for 60 minutes. Stir occasionally. Add the pound of peeled, deveined, and shelled shrimp, 2 cups of shucked oysters, and the cup of crabmeat, cover and cook for 5 minutes. Turn the burner off and allow it to stand for ten more minutes. Serve hot.

Makes 8 servings.

Chicken Salad

This is a very simple, yet filling recipe for chicken salad, excellent for lunch or supper.

What You'll Need:

1 apple (cored, peeled, diced)
1 chicken breast (boneless, skinless, cooked, shredded)
1 cup of pecans (chopped)
2/3 cup of raisins
1/4 cup of celery (chopped)
1/4 cup of onions (chopped)
3 tablespoons of mayonnaise
1 tablespoon of dill pickle relish
salt and pepper

How to Make It:

Combine the 3 tablespoons of mayonnaise with the tablespoon of dill pickle relish and dashes of salt and pepper, using a whisk. In a separate bowl, add the cored, peeled, and diced apple, shredded chicken breast, cup of chopped pecans, 2/3 cup of raisins, 1/4 cup of chopped celery, and 1/4 chopped onions and toss to combine. Pour the mayonnaise dressing over it and toss to coat evenly. Chill for at least half an hour before serving. Serve with lettuce, bread, or crackers.

Makes 6 servings.

Chicken Curry

Chicken curry is a favorite among many and completely grain free.

What You'll Need:

2 pounds of chicken breasts (boneless, skinless, chunked)
1 1/2 cup of onions (chopped)
1/4 cup of olive oil
1 bay leaf
3 tablespoons of curry powder
1 tablespoon of lemon juice
1 tablespoon of tomato paste
1 teaspoon of garlic (minced)
1 teaspoon of cinnamon (ground)
1 teaspoon of paprika
1/2 teaspoon of cayenne pepper
1/2 teaspoon of sugar (granulated)
1/4 teaspoon of ginger (ground)
salt
water

How to Make It:

Pour the 1/4 cup of olive oil in a skillet and turn to

medium high heat. Add the 1 1/2 cup of chopped onions and sauté. Stir in the teaspoon of ground cinnamon and add the bay leaf. Stir in the 3 tablespoons of curry powder, teaspoon of minced garlic, teaspoon of paprika, 1/2 teaspoon of granulated sugar, 1/4 teaspoon of ground ginger, and a few dashes of salt. Cook for a couple of minutes, until the mixture thickens. Stir in the 2 pounds of boneless, skinless, chunked chicken breasts and the tablespoon of tomato paste. Add water until all the chicken is completely covered. Stir and cook on medium low for 20 minutes. Add the tablespoons of lemon juice and the 1/2 teaspoon of cayenne pepper before serving.

Makes 6 servings.

Californian Chicken Soup

This is a delicious soup with avocados, Monterey Jack cheese, and a lot of flavor to make you think of California.

What You'll Need:

2 cans of green chili peppers (4.5 oz. each, drained, diced)
1 can of garbanzo beans (15 oz., drained)
2 chipotle peppers in adobo sauce (minced)
1 avocado (peeled, pitted, sliced)
4 cups of chicken broth
2 cups of chicken (cooked and shredded)
1 cup of rice (white, cooked)
1 cup of Monterey Jack cheese (shredded)
1 teaspoon of oregano (dried)
salt and pepper

How to Make It:

Add the 4 cups of chicken broth to a large soup pot, turn to medium high and just before it boils, turn to low. Add the can of garbanzo beans, 2 minced chipotle peppers , 2 cups of cooked shredded chicken, cup of cooked white rice, and salt and pepper. Simmer on medium low for half an hour. If the soup is too thick, add more chicken broth. Serve by spooning into bowls and topping with a slice of avocado and some shredded Monterey cheese.

Makes 6 servings.

Beef Stew

An all-time favorite, beef stew is the ultimate in comfort foods.

What You'll Need:

2 pounds of beef stew
2 cups of water (divided)
1 1/2 cups of carrots (sliced)
1 1/2 cups of celery (chopped)
1/2 cup of onions (sliced)
1 bay leaf
2 tablespoons of canola oil
2 tablespoons of cornstarch
1 tablespoon of Worcestershire sauce
1 teaspoon of salt
1 teaspoon of sugar (granulated)
1/2 teaspoon of black pepper
1/2 teaspoon of paprika
1/2 teaspoon of garlic (minced)
Dash of allspice (ground)

How to Make It:

Add the 2 tablespoons of canola oil to a skillet and turn the heat to medium high. Add the 2 pounds of stew meat and brown all sides. Transfer the meat to a large pot and add the 1 3/4 cups of water, 1/2 cup of sliced onions, 1 tablespoon of Worcestershire sauce, teaspoon of salt, teaspoon of granulated sugar, 1/2 teaspoon of black pepper, 1/2 teaspoon of paprika, 1/2 teaspoon of minced garlic, and a dash of ground allspice and stir. Drop in the bay leaf, cover and reduce heat to low and simmer for 90 minutes. Remove and discard the bay leaf. Add the 1 1/2 cups of sliced carrots and the 1 1/2 cups of chopped celery, replace the cover and cook for another 40 minutes. Mix 1/4 cup of remaining water with the 2 tablespoons of cornstarch with a whisk. Pour into the stew, stir, and turn heat up to medium high. Stir and cook until it starts to boil, then turn it off and cool to serve.

Makes 6 servings.

Baked Salmon

Salmon is a very healthy food to eat giving the body a good supply of Omega 3 fatty acids. This recipe is a delicious means of giving the body what it needs to stay healthy.

What You'll Need:

4 salmon filets
1 can of tomatoes (chopped, drained, 14 oz.)
3/4 cup of onions (chopped)
2 1/2 tablespoons of olive oil (divided)
2 tablespoons of lemon juice
1 teaspoon of oregano (dried)
1 teaspoon of thyme (dried)
Salt and pepper

How to Make It:

Prep: Preheat oven to degrees Fahrenheit.

Lay the salmon out and drizzle with 1/2 tablespoon of olive oil and sprinkle with salt and pepper. In a bowl, combine the drained can of tomatoes, 3/4 cup of chopped onions, 2 tablespoons of lemon juice, 2 tablespoons of olive oil, teaspoon of dried oregano, and teaspoon of dried thyme. Use a baking sheet that will hold all four fillets, place a sheet of foil down in the bottom, leave it loose. Lay each salmon fillet down on the foil, on the side that was oiled, salted and peppered. Next, spoon the seasoned tomatoes over the salmon, evenly covering all fillets. Take another sheet of foil and place over the top of the fillets, and fold over the edges, rolling them up to make a tight seal, sealing all the fillets inside a large foil "packet." Bake for under 30 minutes, until the salmon is cooked.

Makes 4 servings.

Dutch Oven Chili

This chili recipe certainly creates a pot full of comfort food you will want to eat on for a couple of days, because it is that good.

What You'll Need:

1 pound of ground beef (lean)
2 cups of water
1 can of tomatoes (28 oz., crushed)
1 can of black beans (15.5 oz., drained, rinsed)
1 can of kidney beans (15.5 oz., drained, rinsed)
1 can of pinto beans (15.5 oz., drained, rinsed)
1 cup of onions (diced)
1 cup of bell peppers (red, diced)
1/2 cup of carrots (diced)
1 chipotle chili in adobo sauce (seeded, minced)
1 tablespoon of olive oil
2 teaspoons of adobo sauce
2 teaspoons of cumin (ground)
1/2 teaspoons of oregano (dried)
salt and pepper

How to Make It:

Place a Dutch oven on medium heat. Drizzle the

tablespoon of olive oil in the bottom then add the 1 cup of diced onions, 1 cup of diced red bell pepper, and 1/2 cup of diced carrots. Cover the pot, cook, and stir occasionally for 10 minutes or until all the vegetables are tender. Add the 2 teaspoons of ground cumin, and stir for 60 seconds. Add the ground beef, making it crumble as it browns over high heat. Add the 2 cups of water, can of crushed tomatoes, minced chipotle chili pepper, 2 teaspoons of adobo sauce, 1/2 teaspoon of dried oregano, and dashes of salt and pepper. Lay the lid crossways, so it's not completely covered and turn the heat down to low, stirring occasionally for a half an hour. Add the cans of black, kidney and pinto beans, keep the lid the same, stirring once in a while, and cook for another 20 minutes. Salt and pepper to taste.

Makes 8 servings.

5 Day Meal Plan

These are just suggestions of using some of the recipes within this book on a daily basis. You need to include vegetables and fruit and nuts in your diet as well. Always fix extra vegetables and or a salad with supper.

Day 1

Breakfast - Vanilla Yogurt with Fruit Salad

Snack - Nuts

Lunch - Grain free bread sandwich

Snack - Tortilla chips and salsa

Supper - Beef Stew

Dessert - Banana Date Cookies

Day 2

Breakfast - Oven Omelet

Snack - Piece of fruit

Lunch - Shrimp Soup

Snack - nuts

Supper - Seafood Gumbo

Dessert - Classic No Bake Cookies

Day 3

Breakfast - Sweet Potato Breakfast Casserole

Snack - nuts

Lunch - Kale Mango Salad

Snack - piece of fruit

Supper - Stuffed Peppers

Dessert - Ginger cookies

Day 4

Breakfast - Coffee Cake

Snack - piece of fruit

Lunch - Savory Black Bean Salad

Snack - nuts

Supper - Chicken Curry

Dessert - Oatmeal Chocolate Chip Raisin Cookies

Day 5

Breakfast - Breakfast Burrito

Snack - Piece of Fruit

Lunch - Chili and Corn bread

Snack - nuts

Supper - Baked Salmon

Dessert - Raisin Nut Cake

Section 2: Intermittent Fasting Diet

What is the intermittent fasting diet?

This is a diet in which you eat during specified time frames. There are two popular versions of this diet. One being a day to day eat and fast where you eat on day one, fast on day two, and repeat until the desired weight is lost. The other version is a daily fasting, where you eat for a six to eight hour and then fast the rest of the day.

Starting out on the intermittent fasting diet

Please be aware that results from the intermittent diet vary from person to person. Much of the variance depends upon the build of the body, how much fat, and weight need to be lost and how they eat during the diet. Other factors that influence weight loss are lifestyle (do you smoke? drink? eat excessive junk food?), insulin resistance, exercise or not, and work. All these things work towards either making it difficult to lose the weight or to lose it fast. No two people are alike, even if they each desire to lose the same amount of weight. Keeping this in mind helps you to tailor the diet to your own needs.

Intermittent means eating and fasting in chunks of time. You may need to adjust this as you go along, to help deal with other health issues, to speed things along or to help improve health. Be ready to make adjustments and learn how to bend with the changes. Keeping a positive attitude will carry you a long ways in having good success in this diet.

This is a great diet to start for good weight loss. When the weight and fat are gone you can go on a maintenance, where you may still continue to fast, but more on a less restriction.

Other Issues Helped By Intermittent Fasting

If you suffer from any type of insulin or blood sugar problems, the metabolism is improved by fasting, eating in this manner. Eating through a fasting manner helps the body to lower inflammation rates, helps to improve blood pressure, helps to release stress, and helps to boost the immune system. If the immune system is boosted, the body is able to fight off other illnesses and keep you healthy and strong. Because this diet helps also to increase metabolism (especially if you eat the right food) you will have more energy to exercise and your body will have more energy to digest and disperse the foods you eat.

One of the biggest reasons people gain so much weight is they feel the need to eat all the time. This constant eating causes people to grab for the fast, convenient, and high in sugar and salt foods. These foods are responsible for putting a massive amount of weight on those who gorge. The intermittent fasting diet stops this binge eating and helps to creating a habit of eating during the best times of the day.

The Basics of the Intermittent Fasting Diet

The intermittent fasting diet is an extremely flexible diet plan. There are no set rules for doing it other than having a nice solid block of time to fast. As mentioned above one of the methods of fasting involves taking a day or longer of no food, and doing this a couple of times a week. For obvious reasons, this mode is a lot tougher to deal with, as going a solid day without food may be impossible for some people, especially for those with blood sugar issues.

Daily intermittent fasting is better because it does allow for the intake of food on a daily basis. But it also means for a strict window of daily fasting too and this is what helps to facilitate the weight loss. Basically you eat during a six to eight hour time and fast the remainder.

Your lifestyle will directly affect the effectiveness of this diet. Because the diet is flexible, there are no set foods or meals to eat during the six to eight hour window, just to eat. If you are in the habit of consuming a lot of carbohydrates, (sugars, white flours, and basically food with no nutritious value) then your weight loss may not happen or may be very slow. If your lifestyle is very sedentary, it will take longer to lose the weight.

Here is the thing, if you clean up your eating habits and eat foods packed with nutrition, it will give your body the energy to burn to move about more. You will want to exercise and move about more. Your digestive system will also work more efficiently, digesting in a time and manner that will get rid of the fat and calories.

Choosing the Daily Intermittent Fasting

This book is geared to offer recipes for the daily plan. It is easier to follow the daily fasting routine and can be developed into a habit, which will help it to be easier to do. You will break bad habits of needing to binge or gorge on food, because you know that after your six to eight hours, you simply will not eat. Your body will be able to adjust to this much easier, because you will have food in your body daily. If you eat the right foods, your body will have nutrients in which to work to help keep you healthier.

Snacking is the downfall of many who may eat well during the meals but find themselves reaching for foods void of nutrients. Unfortunately, these types of foods are highly addictive, the more we consume them the more our bodies want it. But it is also a habit that is fairly easy to break if you have the will power to do so. This diet stops the constant snacking.

By fasting on a daily basis, you will be more aware of your body. The hope is you will be aware of the foods you eat during the feeding hours, and will choose to consume healthier foods and snacks.

Be Aware Of Issues

If you do not consume enough calories during the feeding window, you can run the risk of reaching a weight loss plateau. This occurs when the body is too restricted from food (remember what we discussed about "starvation mode" above?) This can be avoided by eating the right foods. If you consume junk foods, then your body will not have substantial energy to keep going during the fasting period. If you eat a balance of good complex carbohydrates, proteins, and nutrients, your body can easily sustain the diet and the body during the fasting.

Some people will not be able to do the intermittent fasting diet. Some people have a greater need for more calories and they simply will not perform well unless they are consuming these calories. It is wise to have a physical and make sure your body can handle such a diet. Go over your choices with your health care provider and let them help you to decide whether or not this diet is right and healthy for you.

Making the Intermittent Diet a Success

This diet can be a great success if you do it right. It does take work and dedication though. First thing is to eat right. Choose foods that are healthy and whole during your feeding and avoid junk foods altogether. Eat a good breakfast each morning that will fuel your body to keep it going during the day. Choose healthy snacks. In the sample 5 day meal plan we suggest to eat fruit and nuts to snack. It is okay to drink fruit juice and eat leftovers or a small meal if you would rather. The point is to consume foods like lean meats, fruits, vegetables, and whole grains that help to give the body all the nutrients it needs to function at optimum levels.

Once the feeding window closes, do not consume any more food until the next day. It is okay and encouraged, though, to drink plenty of water throughout the entire day. Water helps to facilitate weight loss and helps to cleanse the body of impurities and toxins. Try drinking water throughout the feeding window as well. It helps with digestion too.

Take up an exercise routine. If your body is moving around it helps to burn more calories. Exercise also helps the body to release endorphins, and these are nature's way of giving you a natural high. Exercise is addictive too, the more you do it the more you will want to do it. The toughest part is starting. Even if you only work out three times a week for thirty minutes each time, you are giving your body a greater chance of fat and weight loss by doing so.

Sample 5 Day Meal Plan

The three meals here are smaller portions than a regular meal. The meals are to be eaten in a 6 to 8 hour time frame, with a 16 to 18 time frame of fasting. During the fasting time, you can have water. It is okay to have more with the meals if you are hungry. Try having a salad with lunch and supper if needed. Drink plenty of water during the day too.

Day One

Breakfast - Tomato Spinach Eggs
Snack - Nuts
Lunch - Edamame and Grilled Salmon
Snack - Fruit
Supper - Apple and Turkey Ham Salad

Day Two

Breakfast - Whole Grain Hot Cereal with Cherries
Snack - Nuts
Lunch - Balsamic Turkey Meatloaf
Snack - Fruit
Supper - Broccoli Cheese Soup

Day Three

Breakfast - Savory Hash Browns
Snack - Nuts
Lunch Buffalo Chicken with Slaw
Snack - Fruit
Supper - Open Face Tomato and Mozzarella Herb

Sandwich

Day Four

Breakfast - Mexican Breakfast Casserole

Snack - Nuts

Lunch - Shrimp Scampi

Snack - Fruit

Supper - Spinach Salad with Pomegranate Dressing

Day Five

Breakfast - Healthy Breakfast Burrito

Snack - Nuts

Lunch - Italian Chicken

Snack - Fruit

Supper - Baked Potatoes Twice

Intermittent Fasting Diet Recipes

Intermittent Fasting Diet Breakfast Recipes

Breakfast Casserole

This makes a perfect brunch because it is a hearty and filling casserole of eggs, cheese, tomatoes, and English muffins. This recipe needs to be prepared the night before. Makes 8 servings.

What You'll Need:

4 English muffins (halved, toasted)
4 scallions (cut into long bite-sized pieces)
4 eggs plus 3 egg whites
3 cups of milk (low fat)
2/3 cup of cheddar cheese (extra sharp, shredded, divided)
3/4 cup of deli ham (torn, thin slices)
1/2 cup of tomatoes (no oil, sundried, sliced)
1 tablespoon of Dijon mustard
Salt and pepper

How to Make It:

Spray a 2-quart baking dish with cooking spray. Layer the bottom of the pan with the 4 halved and toasted English muffins and the 3/4 cup of torn thin sliced deli ham, making sure to lay it out evenly.   Next layer it with the 4 scallions cut into bite-sized pieces, 1/2 cup of sliced sundried tomatoes, and 1/3 cup of shredded extra sharp cheddar cheese. In a bowl, crack the 4 eggs and add the 3 egg whites and beat with a whisk, then combine with the 3 cups of low fat milk, tablespoon of Dijon mustard and dashes of salt and pepper. Pour the egg mixture over the layered casserole in the baking dish. Add the remaining 1/3 cup of extra sharp cheddar cheese on top. Cover tightly with plastic wrap and refrigerate overnight. Next morning, preheat the oven to 350 degrees Fahrenheit. Remove the plastic wrap and cook the casserole (with a baking sheet under it) for 60 minutes. Remove from oven and let it sit for at least 10 minutes to set and cool before serving and enjoying.

Healthy Breakfast Burrito

Mornings are the time to refuel for the day. Start the day right with a breakfast burrito that is as healthy as it is delicious. Makes 4 servings.

What You'll Need:

4 tortillas (whole wheat, burrito)
4 eggs
4 egg whites
1 avocado (cubed)
1 cup of onions (diced)
1 cup of black beans (cooked, rinsed)
3/4 cup of tomatoes (diced)
1/2 cup of bell peppers (red, seeded, diced)
1/3 cup of pepper Jack cheese (shredded)
1/4 cup of sour cream
1/4 cup of salsa
2 teaspoons of canola oil
1/4 teaspoon of red pepper flakes
Salt and pepper
Hot sauce

How to Make It:

Add the 2 teaspoons of canola oil to a skillet on medium

high heat. Sauté the 1/2 cup of seeded, diced red bell peppers and 1/2 cup of diced onions. Stir in the cup of cooked, rinsed black beans and the 1/4 teaspoon of red pepper flakes. Cook for a couple of minutes to warm, and then add dashes of salt and pepper. Put the contents into a bowl and set aside. In a separate bowl crack the 4 eggs and add the additional 4 egg whites and whisk. Add the 1/3 cup of shredded pepper Jack cheese. Spray the same skillet with cooking spray, heat to medium and scramble the eggs until done. In a separate non-stick skillet, heat to medium, and warm each tortilla on each side for about 30 seconds. Next, to build the burrito, add 1/4 of the sour cream and 1/4 of the salsa followed by 1/4 of the black beans and topped with 1/4 of the eggs and then season with extra salt, pepper, and hot sauce. Roll up and serve. Do this with each one.

Mexican Style Eggs "Huevos Rancheros"

If you love Mexican food, you will love your breakfast fixed fiesta style. Makes 4 servings.

What You'll Need:

4 eggs

4 tortillas (corn, 6 inch, warmed)

1 can of black beans (15.5 oz, drained, rinsed)

1 jalapeno pepper (minced)

1 1/2 cups of tomatoes (fine chopped)

1/2 cup of onions (fine chopped)

1/2 cup of feta cheese (crumbled)

1/2 cup of water (warm)

1/4 cup of cilantro (fresh chopped)

2 tablespoons of olive oil (plus 2 teaspoons, extra virgin)

1 teaspoon of garlic (minced)

1 teaspoon of cumin (ground)

1/2 teaspoon of hot sauce

Salt and pepper

How to Make It:

Mix the 1 jalapeno pepper (minced), 1 1/2 cups of tomatoes (fine chopped), 1/2 cup of onions (fine chopped), 1 teaspoon of garlic (minced), 1 teaspoon of

cumin (ground), 1/2 teaspoon of hot sauce, and dashes
of salt and pepper together to make salsa. Pour 2
teaspoons of olive oil into a skillet and heat to medium
low. Pour in the "salsa" mixture and stir for a couple of
minutes until it thickens. Pour the salsa in a bowl and
set to the side. Add the can of drained, rinsed black
beans along with 1/2 cup of warm water and another
dash of salt into the skillet. Cover, turn heat to low and
simmer while preparing the rest of the eggs. Add the 2
tablespoons of extra virgin olive oil to another skillet and
heat to medium. Crack the eggs, one at a time to make
4 fried eggs, or sunny side up. Season with salt and
pepper. Warm the 4 tortillas by placing on a plate with a
damp paper towel on top and microwave for about 20
seconds. Next, place a tortilla on 4 plates. Equally
divide the beans on top of the 4 tortillas. Add a fried egg
to each one. Add a spoon of salsa on top of each egg,
and then divide the 1/2 cup of feta cheese crumbles on
top of the salsa. Garnish with the 1/4 cup of fresh
chopped cilantro and the rest of the salsa. Serve
immediately.

Mexican Breakfast Casserole

Here is a casserole filled with the spiciness of chili and cilantro, delicious and filling. Makes 6 servings.

What You'll Need:

4 cups of tortilla chips (baked, divided)
4 eggs plus 6 extra egg whites
1 can of green chilies (chopped, drained)
1/2 cup of cheddar cheese (sharp, shredded - divided)
1/2 cup of pepper Jack cheese (shredded - divided)
1/2 cup of salsa (green Verde)
1/4 cup of skim milk
1 tablespoon of cilantro (fresh chopped plus more for garnishment)
3/4 teaspoon of ancho chili powder
Dollops of sour cream
Salt and pepper

How to Make It:

Prep: Preheat the oven to 375 degrees Fahrenheit. Spray a 2 quart baking dish with cooking spray.

Crumble the 4 cups of baked tortilla chips (large crumbles) and lay 2 cups of chips in the bottom of the baking dish. In a bowl, crack the 4 eggs and add the 6 egg whites and beat with a whisk. Add the 1/4 cup of skim milk, 3/4 teaspoon of ancho chili powder, and dashes of salt and pepper and stir. Mix in the can of chopped drained green chilies, 1/4 cup of shredded sharp cheddar cheese, 1/4 cup of shredded pepper Jack cheese, and the tablespoon of fresh chopped cilantro. Pour the mixture over the baked tortilla chips in the baking dish. Place in hot oven and bake for about 22 minutes, until the eggs are set. Pull out of oven and sprinkle the remaining 1/4 cup of shredded sharp cheddar cheese and the 1/4 cup of shredded pepper Jack cheese and place back in the oven for 10 more minutes. Pull from oven, turn heat off, and allow sitting for another 10 minutes. Serve with a spoon of green Verde salsa, dollop of sour cream, and a garnishment of cilantro leaf.

Savory Hash Browns

All you need to do is cook up and egg and have a piece of whole grain toast and you are set for a meal. Makes 4 servings.

What You'll Need:

2 potatoes (Yukon gold, washed, grated - with skins)
2 scallions (chopped)
1 parsnip (peeled, grated)
2 tablespoons of parsley (minced flat leaf)
1 tablespoon of olive oil (extra virgin, divided)
Salt and pepper

How to Make It:

Toss the 2 grated potatoes with the grated parsnip, add the 2 chopped scallions, greens and all. Season with dashes of salt and pepper. Pour the 1/2 tablespoon of extra virgin olive oil into a skillet and heat to medium. Stir in the grated potatoes, parsnips, and scallions, tossing to coat with oil, then press down into the skillet, once in a while, run the spatula under the mixture to prevent sticking. Cook until crispy brown for around 10 minutes. Flip the mixture out onto a large dinner plate. Add the remaining 1/2 tablespoon of olive oil, return skillet to heat, then replace the mixture, uncooked side down to crisp the other side, another 10 minutes. Serve hot.

Squash, Zucchini and Eggs

This is a great summer meal using fresh squash if possible. Makes 6 servings.

What You'll Need:

6 eggs
4 scallions (sliced thin, greens separated out)
3 squash (grated)
3 zucchini (grated)
1 jalapeno (seeded, minced)
1/4 cup of cheddar cheese (sharp white, shredded)
1/4 cup of pepper jack (shredded)
3 tablespoons of parsley (fresh chopped)
2 tablespoons of olive oil (extra virgin)
1 tablespoon of butter
1 tablespoon of salt
1/4 teaspoon of nutmeg (ground)
Salt and pepper

How to Make It:

Toss the 3 shredded squash and the 3 grated zucchinis with a tablespoon of salt while they rest in a colander for 35 minutes. Using a paper towel, squeeze the squash and zucchini.

Preheat the oven to 375 degrees Fahrenheit. Place an oven proof (cast iron works well) skillet on the stove on medium high heat. Pour in the 2 tablespoons of extra virgin olive oil. Reserve 3 tablespoons of the greens from the 4 scallions and put the remainder of the greens and all the whites into the heated oil along with the seeded minced jalapeno and sauté. Toss in the grated squash and zucchini, stir, and toss for about 7 minutes. Add the 3 tablespoons of fresh chopped parsley, 1/4 teaspoon of ground nutmeg, and dashes of salt, pepper, and stir, cooking for another minute. Remove skillet from the stove and sit for 5 minutes away from the heat. Next, pat the squash, zucchini mixture down, then with the back of a serving spoon make 6 indentions, spaced evenly over the squash and zucchini. Place 1/2 of a teaspoon of butter into each of the 6 indentions. Carefully, crack an egg in a cup, then pour right into and indention, with all 6 eggs. Sprinkle dashes of salt and pepper over the eggs. Add the remaining 1/4 cups of shredded sharp cheddar cheese and pepper Jack cheese, evenly over the top. Carefully place the skillet in the hot oven and bake for about 11 minutes. Garnish with the 3 tablespoons of the chopped green scallions and serve immediately.

Tomato Spinach Eggs

This is a delicious way to get protein and vegetables first thing in the morning, with this savory eggs Benedict recipe. Makes 4 servings.

What You'll Need:

8 cups of spinach (fresh baby)
4 slices of tomato (large slices)
4 eggs
2 English Muffins (split in half)
1/2 cup of onions (thin sliced)
1/3 cup of Canadian bacon (chunked)
1/4 cup of vinegar (white distilled)
2 tablespoons of mayonnaise
1 tablespoon of water (warm)
1 tablespoon of olive oil
2 teaspoons of mustard
1 teaspoon of lemon juice
Dash of cayenne pepper
Pepper

How to Make It:

Make the sauce by combining the 2 tablespoons of mayonnaise, 1 tablespoon of water (warm), 2 teaspoons of mustard, 1 teaspoon of lemon juice, and dash of cayenne pepper with a whisk.

Next, start the Benedict eggs by adding several inches of water to a large saucepan. Pour in the 1/4 cup of white distilled vinegar and turn the heat to medium.

Set a nonstick frying pan on medium high, add the tablespoon of olive oil, 1/3 cup of Canadian bacon chunks, and the 1/2 cup of onions, and cook until heated through. Stir in the 8 cups of fresh baby spinach, take the frying pan off the heat, and continue stirring for a couple of minutes until the leaves wilt. Sprinkle pepper and toss.

Pop the English muffins into a toaster to toast lightly on all sides. Set them on a serving platter and top with a slice of tomato. Add 1/4 of the Canadian bacon mixture on top of each tomato slice.

Next, cook one egg at a time, buy cracking into a small dish, then pouring into the simmering vinegar water. Cook for about 4 minutes. Remove and place on top of the Canadian bacon on the English muffin halves. Do this with all 4 eggs. Spoon the hollandaise sauce over the top and serve hot.

Whole Grain Hot Cereal with Cherries

There is nothing heartier than a bowl of hot whole grain cereal first thing in the morning. You will enjoy this meal with the aroma and flavor of fruit making it a delightful meal. Makes 4 servings.

What You'll Need:

5 cups of water
1/2 cup of rice (wild)
1/2 cup of oats (steel-cut)
1/2 cup of wheat cereal (cream of wheat)
1/4 cup of pearl barley
1/4 cup of cherries (dried)
1 cinnamon stick
1 1/2 tablespoons of brown sugar (packed)
1/2 teaspoon of orange zest
1/4 teaspoon of salt
Walnuts (chopped)
Butter
Milk

How to Make It:

The evening before add the 5 cups of water, 1/2 cup of rice (wild), 1/2 cup of oats (steel-cut), 1/2 cup of wheat cereal (cream of wheat), 1/4 cup of pearl barley, 1/4 cup of cherries (dried), 1 cinnamon stick, 1 1/2 tablespoons of brown sugar (packed), 1/2 teaspoon of orange zest, and 1/4 teaspoon of salt and stir in a large sauce pan. Place the cover and let sit on the stove with the heat off over night. The morning of breakfast, turn the stove on high and bring to a boil, then turn it down on low to simmer, cover on for 20 minutes. Keep the cover on, turn the stove off and let it sit for another 5 minutes. Serve in bowls and garnish with chopped walnuts, butter and milk if desired.

Whole Wheat Pancakes with Apples

Pancakes are always fun to cook and eat. You cannot go wrong with this recipe, which uses whole-wheat flour to give you the benefit of whole grains, and the goodness of fresh apples. Makes 6 servings.

What You'll Need:

1 cup of buttermilk (low fat)
3/4 cup of skim milk
3/4 cup of apples (cored, diced)
3/4 cup of flour (all-purpose)
3/4 cup of flour (whole-wheat)
2 eggs
6 tablespoons of maple syrup
1 tablespoon of honey
2 teaspoons of baking powder
1/2 teaspoon of baking soda
1/4 teaspoon of salt

How to Make It:

Prep: Preheat the oven to 250 degrees Fahrenheit.

In a bowl, combine the 3/4 cup of flour (all-purpose), 3/4 cup of flour (whole-wheat), 2 teaspoons of baking powder, 1/2 teaspoon of baking soda, and 1/4 teaspoon of salt. Crack the 2 eggs and beat with a whisk in a cup. In a separate bowl, combine the 1-cup of buttermilk (low fat), 3/4 cup of skim milk, beaten eggs, and the tablespoon of honey. Gradually add the dry ingredients, do not over stir.

Next, place the diced apples in a microwave safe dish, cover with plastic wrap, and microwave on normal for 2 minutes to soften.

Turn the heat to medium on a non-stick skillet or griddle. Ladle out about a fourth a cup of batter onto the hot surface. Spoon a couple of apples over the top, flip after a couple of minutes. Repeat until all the batter and apples are gone. Drizzle with the maple syrup or your favorite syrup over the top, or sprinkle cinnamon and sugar over the top.

Zucchini Frittata

This delicious breakfast would make a good dinner choice too, as it's healthy and filling, full of feta cheese, zucchini, potatoes and turkey bacon. Makes 4 servings.

What You'll Need:

4 eggs + 2 egg whites
2 strips of turkey bacon (cooked, crumbled)
1 zucchini (grated and dried with a towel)
1 cup of potatoes (russet, cubed)
1/2 cup of feta cheese
1/2 cup of onion (chopped fine)
2 tablespoons of cilantro (fresh chopped)
1 tablespoon of olive oil
3/4 teaspoon of salt
1/2 teaspoon of garlic (minced)
1/4 teaspoon of hot sauce

How to Make It:

Add the 1 cup of cubed potatoes to a saucepan and cover with water, bring to a boil on high heat, then turn down to medium high. Cook for about 7 minutes or until the potatoes are tender enough to eat. Remove from heat, drain the water and place in a bowl. Using a paper towel, dry the potato cubes.

In a bowl, add the 4 eggs and 2 egg whites and beat with a whisk. Stir in the cup of cilantro, 3/4 teaspoon of salt, and 1/4 teaspoon of hot sauce.

Turn the on the oven broiler to high.

Place an ovenproof skillet on the stove (about a 10 inch size) and turn to medium high heat. Add the tablespoon of olive oil and sauté the 1/2 cup of fine chopped onion and the 1/2 teaspoon of minced garlic. Stir in the grated zucchini and cook for another 5 minutes. Stir in the cooked potato cubes, browning them for about 4 minutes. Next, pour the whisked egg mixture over the potatoes and zucchini. Place the skillet back on medium heat, lifting the edges to allow the egg to run, for a couple of minutes. Next, sprinkle the 2 strips of crumbled turkey bacon and the 1/2 cup of feta cheese over the top and place under the broiler for 5 minutes. Serve hot.

Intermittent Fasting Diet Dinner Recipes

Balsamic Turkey Meatloaf

If you are a meatloaf lover you will enjoy this different twist for meatloaf, which is a bit healthier than the beef counterpart. Makes 8 servings.

What You'll Need:

1.5 pounds of ground turkey
1 zucchini (fine diced)
1 bell pepper (red fine diced)
1 bell pepper (yellow fine diced)
1 egg
1 cup of bread crumbs
3/4 cup of ketchup (divided)
1/4 cup + 2 tablespoons of balsamic vinegar
1/4 cup of Parmesan cheese (grated)
1/4 cup of Romano cheese (grated)
1/4 cup of parsley (fresh chopped)
2 tablespoons of olive oil (extra-virgin)
1 tablespoon of thyme (fresh fine chopped)
2 1/2 teaspoons of garlic (minced)
1/2 teaspoon of red pepper flakes
Salt and pepper

How to Make It:

Prep: Preheat oven to 425 degrees Fahrenheit. Line a 9x5 inch loaf pan with foil.

Add the 2 tablespoons of extra virgin olive oil to a skillet on high heat and sauté the fine diced zucchini, red and yellow bell peppers, 2 1/2 teaspoons of minced garlic and dashes of salt and pepper for about 5 minutes. Set aside.

Crack the egg in a bowl and beat with a whisk, and stir in the 1/4 cup of fresh chopped parsley and the tablespoon of fresh fine chopped thyme. Add the 1.5 pounds of ground turkey, breaking it up with your hands, along with the cup of breadcrumbs, 1/4 cup of grated Parmesan cheese, 1/4 cup of grated Romano cheese, 1/2 cup of ketchup, 2 tablespoons of balsamic vinegar, and the zucchini and bell peppers.   Mix with bare hands and mold into a loaf. Add to the lined loaf pan. Make the sauce for the topping by mixing the 1/4 cup of ketchup with the 1/4 cup of balsamic vinegar and the 1/2 teaspoon of red pepper flakes, and dashes of salt and pepper. Stir with a whisk, and then pour over the top of the meat loaf. Cook for 1 hour and 15 minutes, until the internal temperature of the meatloaf reaches 165 degrees Fahrenheit with a meat thermometer.

Buffalo Chicken with Slaw

Buffalo chicken is always associated as an appetizer but here it is a delicious main meal with a side of fresh homemade slaw. Makes 4 servings.

What You'll Need:

4 chicken breast halves (boneless, skinless, cut into strips)
4 cups of cabbage (shredded)
2 cups of buttermilk
2 cups of carrots (grated)
2 cups of bread crumbs (fine)
1 cup of celery (thin sliced)
1/2 cup of canola oil
1/2 cup of mayonnaise
1/2 cup of sour cream
1/2 cup of blue cheese (crumbles)
2 tablespoons of hot sauce (divided)
Salt and pepper

How to Make It:

Combine the 2 cups of buttermilk with 1 tablespoon of hot sauce and dashes of salt and pepper. Put the 4 boneless, skinless chicken breast halves cut into strips into a shallow dish. Pour the buttermilk mixture over the chicken, cover and refrigerate for 60 minutes. Combine the 1/2 cup of mayonnaise with the 1/2 cup of sour cream and the 1/2 cup of blue cheese crumbles in a blender or food processor until nice and lump free (this is the dressing). Using a whisk, add the remaining tablespoon of hot sauce and mix. In a bowl, add the 4 cups of shredded cabbage, 2 cups of grated carrots, with the 1 cup of thin sliced celery and toss. Pour 3/4 cup of the dressing over the cabbage mixture and toss to coat all. There will be 1/4 cup of dressing left over for a dipping sauce.

Add the 2 cups of fine bread crumbs to a shallow dish. Shake each chicken strip from the marinade and roll in the bread crumbs. Pour the 1/2 cup of canola oil into a skillet and turn to medium high heat. Fry each coated chicken strip for 4 minutes, turn and cook another 4 minutes, until all the chicken is cooked.

Serve with a side of slaw and dip in the dressing.

Edamame and Grilled Salmon

It is hard to beat salmon in terms of nutrition and flavor. This delicious meal is savory to the palate the filling. Makes 4 servings.

What You'll Need:

4 salmon fillets (skin on)
2 scallions (fine chopped)
1 1/3 cup of Edamame (cooked)
1/4 cup of cilantro leaves (fresh fine chopped)
2 teaspoons of canola oil
2 teaspoons of lime juice
2 teaspoons of soy sauce
2 teaspoons of honey
1 teaspoon of ginger (grated)
1/4 teaspoon of sesame seeds (black)
Salt and pepper
lime wedges (for garnish)

How to Make It:

Prep: Preheat the grill to medium high. Rub canola oil on the grates.

Mix the 2 fine chopped scallions with the 1/4 cup of

fresh fine chopped cilantro leaves, 2 teaspoons of canola oil, and the teaspoon of grated ginger. Dash salt and pepper and toss. Cut into the middle of the skins of the salmon fillets, making 2 slits about three inches in length from top to bottom, cutting halfway into the salmon. Do so with each fillet, and evenly spoon the scallions and cilantro into each slit. Salt and pepper the rest of the salmon fillets. In a cup, mix the 2 teaspoons of lime juice, 2 teaspoons of soy sauce, with the 2 teaspoons of honey with a whisk. Gently set each salmon fillet on the grill with the skin / herbs side facing up. Grill for about 3 1/2 minutes. Flip the salmon, brush the top with the lime juice sauce mixture and grill for another 3 1/2 minutes. Place cooked salmon fillets on a serving platter; evenly sprinkle the 1/4 teaspoon of black sesame seeds over the tops. Garnish with the lime wedges and serve with the 1 1/3 cup of cooked Edamame in a serving dish.

Grilled Chicken Tostadas

This is a healthy meal made with tasty seasoned chicken breasts and a variety of other savory flavors. Makes 4 servings.

What You'll Need:

4 tortillas (flour, 8 inch)
2 chicken breasts (boneless, skinless, cut into bite-sized pieces)
1 pound of tomatillos (husked and rinsed)
4 lime wedges
1 chipotle chili in adobo sauce (chopped coarse)
2 cups of romaine lettuce (shredded)
1/3 cup of feta cheese (crumbled)
1/4 cup of lime juice
4 tablespoons of onions (fine chopped)
2 tablespoons of cilantro (fresh chopped)
1 tablespoon of olive oil
1 teaspoon of garlic (minced)
Salt

How to Make It:

In a large bowl, combine the 1/4 cup of lime juice with the coarse chopped chipotle chili in adobo sauce and dashes of salt. Toss in the 2 cut up boneless, skinless chicken breasts and cover. Refrigerate for 2 hours to marinate. Place the chicken pieces on greased skewers. Turn the grill to medium heat. Spray the 4 8-inch flour tortillas with cooking spray and grill them for about 45 seconds, flip and grill another 45 seconds. Place the skewered chicken and the pound of husked, rinsed tomatillos on the grill and turn every 30 seconds for about 5 minutes. Remove the chicken and tomatillos from the heat. Remove the skewers from the chicken. Chop the grilled tomatillos into bite sized chunks in a bowl. Add the tablespoon of olive oil and a dash of salt and toss.   Layer the tostadas by placing a tortilla down first, then divide the 2 cups of shredded romaine lettuce, tomatillos, chicken, 4 tablespoons of onions (fine chopped), and the 2 tablespoons of cilantro (fresh chopped). Garnish each plate with a lime wedge. Enjoy.

Italian Chicken

This savory Italian Chicken dish goes well with a salad or steamed vegetables. Makes 6 servings.

What You'll Need:

4 chicken breast halves (bone- in, skinless)
2 chicken thighs (skinless, bone-in)
1 can of tomatoes (diced, 15 oz)
3 oz of prosciutto (chopped)
1/2 cup of white grape juice
1/2 cup of chicken stock
1/2 cup of bell pepper (red, sliced)
1/2 cup of bell pepper (yellow, sliced)
1/4 cup of olive oil
1/4 cup of parsley (fresh flat leaf, chopped)
2 tablespoons of capers
1 tablespoon of thyme (fresh)
1 1/2 teaspoon of salt (divided)
1 teaspoon of oregano (fresh)
1 teaspoon of garlic (minced)
1/2 teaspoon of pepper

How to Make It:

Rinse and pat dry the chicken. Rub 1/2 teaspoons each

of salt and pepper on all of the chicken. Pour the 1/4 cup of olive oil in a skillet and turn to medium heat. Add the chicken to the hot oil and brown on each side. Place on a platter and set to the side. In the same skillet add the 1/2 cups of chopped yellow and red bell peppers and the 3 oz of chopped prosciutto and sauté. Stir in the teaspoon of minced garlic and cook for another 60 seconds. Add the 15 oz can of diced tomatoes, 1/2 cup of white grape juice, 1 tablespoon of thyme (fresh), 1 1/2 teaspoon of salt (divided), 1 teaspoon of oregano (fresh), and 1 teaspoon of garlic (minced). Deglaze the skillet by scraping the bits from the bottom into the mixture. Add the cooked chicken and pout in the 1/2 cup of chicken stock. Turn the heat to high and bring to a boil. Cover, reduce the heat to low and simmer for about 25 minutes. When cooked, stir in the 1/4 cup of fresh chopped flat leaf parsley and the 2 tablespoons of capers, then serve.

Oriental Turkey Burgers

Here is a different twist to an American favorite, turkey burgers seasoned up with oriental spices. Makes 4 burgers.

What You'll Need:

12 oz of ground turkey
4 hamburger buns (whole grain)
2 scallions (chopped)
1/2 cup of water (boiling)
1/2 cup of English cucumber (sliced thin)
1/4 cup of balsamic vinegar
1/4 cup of bulgur wheat
1/4 cup of yogurt (plain)
1/4 cup of cilantro (fresh whole)
1/8 cup of onion (sliced thin)
2 tablespoons of hoisin sauce
2 tablespoons of cilantro (fresh chopped)
2 teaspoons of canola oil
1 teaspoon of sugar (granulated)
1 teaspoon of ginger (grated)
1 teaspoon of chili garlic sauce
1/2 teaspoon of garlic (minced)
Salt and pepper

How to Make It:

First, combine the 1/2 cup of boiling water with the 1/4 cup of bulgur wheat in a small bowl. Seal with plastic wrap and set aside for about 50 minutes. Next, using a whisk in a separate bowl mix the 1/4 cup of balsamic vinegar with the teaspoon of granulated sugar. Toss in the 1/2 cup of thin sliced English cucumber and the 1/8 cup of thin sliced onions. Sprinkle with dashes of salt and pepper. Cover and set in refrigerator for half an hour. In another bowl, whisk together the 1/4 cup of plain yogurt with the teaspoon of chili garlic sauce and more dashes of salt and pepper.   Set the bowl aside while preparing the turkey. When the bulgur wheat is ready, drain the water and add the 12 oz of ground turkey, 2 chopped scallions, 2 tablespoons of hoisin sauce, 2 tablespoons of fresh chopped cilantro, teaspoon of grated ginger, and the 1/2 teaspoon of minced garlic. Mix with bare hands to insure good mixture. Separate into 4 patties. Add the 2 teaspoons of canola oil to a skillet and heat to medium high. Cook the turkey burgers until well done, 4 minutes on each side. Next, pour the cucumber mixture into a colander to drain, and then toss in the 1/4 cup of fresh whole cilantro leaves. Create the burgers by spreading the yogurt sauce onto each bun half, add the turkey burger, and then add a spoon of the cucumber cilantro mixture.

Enjoy.

Shrimp Scampi

If you love shrimp, you will love this recipe, complete with whole grain noodles. Makes 4 servings.

What You'll Need:

16 shrimp (large, deveined, shelled)

6 oz of spaghetti noodles (whole grain)

6 black olives (pitted, chopped)

1/2 cup of onions (sliced thin)

1/4 cup of croutons (multi-grain, crumbed)

1/4 cup of parsley (fresh flat leaf, divided)

1/4 cup of chicken stock

1/4 cup of white grape juice

1 1/2 tablespoons of lemon zest (divided)

1 tablespoon of lemon juice

1 tablespoon of olive oil

1/2 teaspoon of garlic (minced)

1/4 teaspoon of red pepper flakes (crushed)

1/4 teaspoon of salt

How to Make It:

Cook the spaghetti noodles according to the directions on the package to "al dente." In a separate bowl, add the 1/4 cup of croutons (multi-grain, crumbed),

1/2 tablespoon of parsley (fresh flat leaf), and a tablespoon of the lemon zest and stir, let sit. Meanwhile, in a skillet, add the tablespoon of olive oil and turn to medium heat. Stir in the 1/2 cup of thin sliced onions, 1/2 teaspoon of garlic (minced), 1/4 teaspoon of red pepper flakes (crushed) and sauté for a minute. Stir in the 16 large deveined and shelled shrimp and the 1/4 teaspoon of salt and cook for another 90 seconds. Add the 1/4 cup of chicken stock, 1/4 cup of white grape juice, tablespoon of lemon juice and the 6 chopped, pitted black olives. Turn heat to high and bring to a boil, stirring and cooking for a minutes, then turn the heat back down to medium. Add the cook spaghetti noodles and the remainder of the parsley and lemon zest. Toss and pour into a serving dish. Sprinkle the 1/4 cup of crumbles multi-grain croutons over the top and serve.

Vegetable Pot Pie

Sometimes you simply do not need meat to make a full meal. This is a perfect tasty pot pie and all the better because it's homemade. Makes 8 servings.

What You'll Need:

2 pie crusts (9-inch deep dish, unbaked, rolled)
1 3/4 cup of vegetable stock
1 cup of carrots (thin sliced)
1 cup of English peas (frozen)
1 cup of potatoes (diced)
2/3 cup of milk
1/2 cup of celery (thin sliced)
1/2 cup of butter
1/3 cup of onion (fine chopped)
1/3 cup of flour (all-purpose, unbleached)
Salt and pepper
1/4 teaspoon of celery seed
1/4 teaspoon of garlic powder
Water

How to Make It:

Prep: Preheat the oven to 425 degrees Fahrenheit.

Place a saucepan over high heat and add 1 cup of carrots (thin sliced), 1 cup of English peas (frozen), 1 cup of potatoes (diced), and 1/2 cup of celery (thin sliced) and add enough water to cover the vegetables and bring the water to a boil. Add a lid and cook for 15 minutes, vegetables are done when they are tender. Drain water and set aside for a few minutes. Place a skillet on medium heat and add the 1/2 cup of butter and sauté the 1/3 cup of fine chopped onions. Add the 1/3 cup of flour (all-purpose, unbleached), dashes of salt and pepper, 1/4 teaspoon of celery seed, and 1/4 teaspoon of garlic powder and stir. Cook until well blended for a couple of minutes. Combine with the 1 3/4 cup of vegetable stock and the 2/3 cup of milk. Turn the heat to medium low and simmer for 5 more minutes. Turn off heat and stir in the cooked vegetables. Unroll a pie crust and place in a 9 inch deep dish pie pan. Add the vegetable mixture into the pie crust. Unroll the other pie crust and carefully place on top of the vegetable pie, sealing the edges but pressing a fork to make small ridges. Cut a couple of slits in the crust to vent the steam while cooking. Place on a baking sheet and in the oven for 35 minutes. Allow to sit to cool for about 10 minutes before serving.

Intermittent Fasting Diet Light Snack Recipes

Apple and Turkey Ham Salad

This is a delightfully crunchy sweet and savory salad. Makes 6 servings.

What You'll Need:

1/2 pound of turkey ham (thin sliced, torn)
4 endives (crosswise sliced)
3 apples (crisp, cored, sliced thin)
2 bunches of trimmed watercress
2 cups of onions (sliced thin)
1/4 cup of sour cream
1/4 cup of water
3 tablespoons of olive oil (extra virgin)
2 tablespoons of lemon juice
2 tablespoons of apple cider vinegar
2 tablespoons of Dijon mustard
Salt and pepper

How to Make It:

Add the 3 thin sliced apples into a bowl, pour over the 2 tablespoons of lemon juice, and toss to coat. Add the 3 tablespoons of extra virgin olive oil to a skillet on medium heat. Stir in the 2 cups of thin sliced onions and dashes of salt and sauté. Add the 2 tablespoons of apple cider vinegar and the 2 tablespoons of Dijon mustard in with the onions and stir with a whisk. Add the 1/4 cups of sour cream and water and continue stirring with the whisk. Pour the dressing over the lemon apples and toss. Toss in the 4 crosswise sliced endives, 2 bunches of trimmed watercress and the 1/2 pound of thin sliced and torn turkey ham. Add dashes of salt and pepper and toss before serving.

Baked Potatoes Twice

Baked potatoes are a tasty light meal, but "twice" baked potatoes are even better! Makes 4 servings.

What You'll Need:

4 potatoes (medium sized russet works best)
1/2 cup of onions (thin sliced)
1/2 cup of cream cheese with chives
1/2 cup of milk
1 tablespoon of butter
1 tablespoon of parsley (fresh chopped, plus 4 pinches)
2 teaspoons of thyme (fresh chopped)
1 teaspoon of canola oil
1 teaspoon of garlic (minced)
Salt and pepper

How to Make It:

Prep: Preheat the oven to 375 degrees Fahrenheit. Wash the potatoes, pat dry, and then rub the outside with the teaspoon of canola oil. Sprinkle salt over them and place in the oven, with a baking sheet on the rack below. Bake for 75 minutes; remove from the oven to cool.

Add the tablespoon of butter to a skillet on medium heat. Stir in the 1/2 cup of thin sliced onions and dashes of salt and pepper for about 7 minutes. Stir in the 2 teaspoons of fresh chopped thyme and the teaspoon of minced garlic, stirring for a minute. Remove from heat. Cut the potatoes in half, lengthwise, leaving the skin intact on the bottom. Carefully scoop the meat of the potato, leaving the skins intact. Place the scooped potatoes into the onion mixture and mix. Combine with the 1/2 cup of cream cheese with chives and the 1/2 cup of milk, the potatoes will be lumpy. Add the tablespoon of fresh chopped parsley and mix well. Evenly spoon the potato mixture back into the potato skins. Place the potato halves on the baking sheet and return to the hot oven for about 23 minutes. Garnish with a pinch of fresh chopped parsley and enjoy.

Broccoli Cheese Soup

Here is a lighter meal, made with wholesome broccoli, savory herbs, and delicious cheese. Makes 4 servings.

What You'll Need:

1 package of broccoli florets (frozen, 16 oz)
3 cups of chicken stock
1 1/4 cups of Cheddar cheese (shredded, sharp)
1 cup of French bread (large cubes)
1 cup of onions (sliced)
1/2 cup of heavy cream
5 tablespoons of butter (divided)
3 tablespoons of flour (all-purpose)
2 tablespoons of olive oil (extra virgin)
1/2 teaspoon of garlic (minced)
1/2 teaspoon of thyme (fresh chopped)
1/4 teaspoon of white pepper (ground)
1/4 teaspoon of Creole seasoning
Salt
Nutmeg

How to Make It:

Add 3 tablespoons of butter to a medium saucepan turn to medium high heat. Sauté the 1 cup of sliced onions and add dashes of salt, nutmeg, and 1/4 teaspoon of ground white pepper. Stir in the 1/2 teaspoon of minced garlic and the 1/2 teaspoon of fresh chopped thyme for several seconds. While stirring with a whisk, sprinkle in the 3 tablespoons of all-purpose flour, keep stirring for about 2 minutes over the heat. Pour in the 3 cups of chicken stock, continue to stir with the whisk until all the lumps are gone. Turn the heat to high to bring to a boil while stirring. Turn the heat to low and simmer for 5 minutes, stirring often. Add the 16 oz package of frozen broccoli florets and cook for another 10 minutes, stirring often. If desired, pour into a blender and food processor to blend. Or stir with a masher, mashing the broccoli. Return to the saucepan on low heat. Preheat the oven to 400 degrees Fahrenheit. Pour in the 1/2 cup of heavy cream, stirring while the cream heats. Pour in the 1 1/4 cups of Cheddar cheese, stirring until melted. Add the last 2 tablespoons of butter, stirring until melted and blended.

Put the 1 cup of large cubed French bread and toss with the 2 tablespoons of extra virgin olive oil and the 1/4 teaspoon of Creole seasoning. Spread on a baking sheet and bake for 3 minutes in the hot oven. Remove to flip the croutons over and bake another 3 minutes.

Ladle soup and top with the croutons to serve.

Cauliflower Soup

Here is a delicious and filling, yet light, soup. Makes 4 servings.

What You'll Need:

1 head of cauliflower (chopped florets)
4 parsley leaves (fresh)
6 cups of chicken stock
1 cup of potatoes (scrubbed, skin-on, cubed)
1/2 cup of milk
1/2 cup of onions (chopped)
1 tablespoon of canola oil
1 teaspoon of butter
Salt and pepper

How to Make It:

Add the tablespoon of canola oil and the teaspoon of butter to a large saucepan over medium low heat. Stir in the 1/2 cup of chopped onions, cook and stir for 10 minutes. Add the heat of chopped cauliflower florets, 6 cups of chicken stock, and the cup of cubed potatoes and season with dashes of salt and pepper. Turn the heat to high and bring liquid to a boil. Turn heat to medium, cover and cook for 20 more minutes, until the vegetables are tender. Pour the soup into a blender or food processor to combine until smooth. Pour back into the saucepan and reheat to medium. Add more salt and pepper to taste. Thick soup may be thinned with extra milk. Garnish with a fresh parsley leaf in each bowl.

Greens with Baked Beans

This is a delicious one dish meal that offers wholesome beans along with smoked turkey ham and savory herbs. Makes 6 servings.

What You'll Need:

1 bunch of greens (mustard greens or Swiss chard, chopped, stems removed)
2 cans of pinto beans (drained, rinsed, 15 oz)
1 can of navy beans (undrained, 15oz)
1 can of tomatoes (crushed 15 oz)
1/2 cup of smoked turkey ham (diced)
1/2 cup of celery (fine chopped)
1/2 cup of carrots (fine chopped)
1/4 cup of parsley (fresh chopped)
1/4 cup of onion (chopped)
1/4 cup of water
1 tablespoon of olive oil (extra virgin)
1 teaspoon of garlic (minced)
1 teaspoon of thyme (fresh chopped)
1 teaspoon of oregano (fresh chopped)
Salt and pepper

How to Make It:

Prep: Preheat oven to 375 degrees Fahrenheit. Place a large skillet on the stove on medium heat and add the tablespoon of olive oil. Stir in and sauté the 1/2 cup of celery (fine chopped), 1/2 cup of carrots (fine chopped), 1/4 cup of onion (chopped), and 1 teaspoon of garlic (minced). Season with salt and pepper. Stir in the bunch of greens along with the 1/2 cup of diced smoked turkey ham and 1/4 cup of water. Cook for 3 minutes. Stir in the can of crushed tomatoes and turn the heat to medium high for 5 minutes. Stir in the 2 cans of drained, rinsed pinto beans, and the can of undrained navy beans. Next add the 1/4 cup of parsley (fresh chopped), 1 teaspoon of thyme (fresh chopped), and the 1 teaspoon of oregano (fresh chopped). Stir and heat through. Using a potato masher, mash the some of the beans (not all). Sprinkle with salt and pepper. Pour into a baking dish (2 quart) and cover with foil. Bake for 55 minutes, removing the foil for the last 10. Allow to cool for about 5 minutes before serving.

Maple Flavored Sweet Potato Fries

Here is a healthy and sweet version of a favorite, a nice alternative to French fries. Makes 6 servings.

What You'll Need:

5 sweet potatoes (peeled and cut into small wedges)
1 tablespoon of canola oil
1 tablespoon of maple syrup
1/2 teaspoon of lemon zest
Salt and pepper
Nutmeg

How to Make It:

Prep: Preheat the oven to 425 degrees Fahrenheit. Line a baking sheet with foil.

Place the sweet potato wedges in a large bowl, add the tablespoon of canola oil, and toss to coach each piece. Add dashes of salt and pepper. Place the wedges on the foil lined baking sheet and place in the hot oven for 20 minutes. Take the baking sheet out of the oven and place the wedges back in the bowl. This time add the tablespoon of maple syrup and toss to coat all. Place the potatoes back on the baking sheet and bake for 7 minutes, then flip the potato wedges and bake another 7 minutes. Add to a serving bowl, toss with the 1/2 teaspoon of lemon zest and dashes of salt, pepper, and nutmeg before serving.

Nutty Cucumber Mango Rice Salad

Enjoy something different made with peanuts, mangos, cucumbers and rice. Makes 6 servings.

What You'll Need:

2 scallions (sliced thin)
1 cucumber (English, diced)
1 jalapeno (red, seeded, diced)
1 1/2 cups of saffron rice
1 cup of mango (chopped)
1/2 cup of cilantro (fresh chopped)
1/3 cup of peanuts (salted, roasted, chopped)
1/4 cup of quinoa (rinsed)
2 tablespoons of lime juice
2 tablespoons of canola oil
1 tablespoon of lime zest
1 teaspoon of sugar (granulated)
Salt and pepper
Water

How to Make It:

Cook the 1 1/2 cups of saffron rice according to the package directions. In another saucepan add water and dashes of water and turn heat to high to bring to a boil.

Stir in the 1/4 cup of rinsed quinoa and turn heat to medium high. Cook for 12 minutes, until it turns tender. Pour into a colander and rinse with cool water and drain. In a separate bowl, combine the 2 tablespoons of lime juice, 2 tablespoons of canola oil, tablespoon of lime zest, teaspoon of granulated sugar and dashes of salt and pepper, using a whisk. Stir in the cook saffron rice, 2 thin sliced scallions, diced English cucumber, seeded and diced red jalapeno, cup of chopped mango, 1/2 cup of fresh chopped cilantro 1/3 cup of salted, roasted, chopped peanuts, and the cooked quinoa. Toss and season with more salt and pepper if desired.

Open Face Tomato and Mozzarella Herb Sandwich

This is a unique twist from a sandwich; there is no meat, just the delicious tomato and smoked Mozzarella with savory herbs on a baguette roll.   Makes 4 servings.

What You'll Need:

4 slices of smoked mozzarella (thick)
4 slices of tomato (thick)
1 demi baguette (4 oz.)
2 tablespoons of parsley (fresh chopped)
1 1/2 tablespoons of Parmesan cheese (fine grated)
2 teaspoons of thyme (fresh chopped)
2 teaspoons of olive oil
1 teaspoon of garlic (minced)
Salt and pepper

How to Make It:

Prep: Preheat the oven to broil.

In a bowl, add the 2 tablespoons of fresh chopped parsley, 2 teaspoons of fresh chopped thyme, teaspoon of minced garlic and 2 teaspoons of olive oil and combine. Slice the baguette lengthwise in two.   Cut in half so you have 4 pieces of bread. Evenly divide and spread the herbs over the bread, face up. Evenly sprinkle the 1 1/2 tablespoons of fine grated Parmesan cheese over the 4 slices. Bake under the broiler for 2 minutes. Remove and add a slice of tomato, and a slice of smoked mozzarella cheese on top of each slice of bread. Return to the broiler long enough for the cheese to melt, about a minute or two. Serve hot.

Orange Stir Fry Vegetables

This is a light dish made with just vegetables with the light fruity flavor of orange. Makes 4 servings.

What You'll Need:

1 can of water chestnuts (drained, 4oz)
1 cup of orange juice
1 cup of celery (chopped)
1 cup of mushrooms (rinsed, sliced)
1/2 cup of bell pepper (red, thin sliced)
1/2 cup of carrots (sliced)
1/2 cup of squash (sliced yellow)
1/2 cup of broccoli (chopped)
1/4 cup of baby corn
1/4 cup of snow peas
1/8 cup of onions (thin sliced)
2 tablespoons of cornstarch
2 tablespoons of orange zest
2 tablespoons of canola oil (divided)
1 tablespoon of soy sauce
1 teaspoon of ginger (chopped)
1 teaspoon of garlic (minced)
Salt
4 orange slices
Cooked rice (enough for 4 servings)

How to Make It:

Pour the cup of orange juice into a bowl and combine with the 2 tablespoons of cornstarch, tablespoon of soy sauce, teaspoon of chopped ginger, teaspoon of minced garlic and dashes of salt. Add a wok or large skillet to high heat and pour in the tablespoon of canola oil and sauté the cup of sliced mushrooms, 1/2 cup of sliced carrots, and the 1/8 cup of thin sliced onions for just one minute. Mix in the 1/2 cup of sliced yellow squash, 1/2 cup of chopped broccoli, and 1/4 cup of snow peas. Stir in the 4 oz can of drained water chestnuts, cup of chopped celery, 1/2 cup of thin sliced red bell peppers, and 1/4 cup of baby corn. Cook for another couple of minutes. Pour in the orange sauce, stir and heat through. Serve over the cooked rice and garnish with the 2 tablespoons of orange zest and an orange slice on each plate.

Parsley Mint Roasted Carrots

This is a delicious way to eat your carrots, and nutritious to boot. Makes 4 servings.

What You'll Need:

2 1/2 cups of carrots (halved lengthwise and cut into 2-inch chunks)
1/2 cup of chicken stock
1/4 cup of mint (fresh chopped)
1/4 cup of parsley (fresh chopped)
4 teaspoons of olive oil
2 teaspoons of lemon juice
1/2 teaspoon of lemon zest
Salt and pepper

How to Make It:

Pour the 1/2 cup of chicken broth in a skillet and turn to medium high heat. Add the 2/12 cups of chunked carrots and a teaspoon of olive oil, stir, and bring to a boil. Place a lid on, reduce heat to medium, and cook for 13 more minutes. Remove the lid, stir and cook off all of the chicken stock and cook the carrots another 3 minutes to slight brown. Add dashes of salt and pepper. In a small bowl mix the 1/4 cup of fresh chopped mint,

1/4 cup of fresh chopped parsley, 2 teaspoons of lemon juice and 1/2 teaspoon of lemon zest. Place the carrots in a serving bowl and toss with the mint, parsley mixture. Serve warm.

Quinoa with Herbs

Quinoa is a super food because of the high levels of nutrients within it. Makes 4 servings.

What You'll Need:

2 3/4 cups of chicken stock
1 1/2 cups of quinoa
3/4 cup of basil (fresh chopped leaves)
1/4 cup of parsley (fresh chopped)
1/2 cup of lemon juice (divided)
1/4 cup of olive oil (extra virgin)
1 tablespoon of thyme (fresh chopped leaves)
2 teaspoons of lemon zest
Salt and pepper

How to Make It:

Pour the 2 3/4 cups of chicken stock into a medium size saucepan along with the 1 1/2 cups of quinoa and the 1/4 cup of lemon juice, turn to medium high heat, and bring to a boil. Place lid on saucepan, turn to low, and simmer for about 14 minutes. Meanwhile, combine the 3/4 cup of basil (fresh chopped leaves), 1/4 cup of parsley (fresh chopped), 1/4 cup of lemon juice (divided), 1/4 cup of olive oil (extra virgin), 1 tablespoon of thyme (fresh chopped leaves), 2 teaspoons of lemon zest, and dashes of salt and pepper in a small bowl. When the quinoa is cooked, add to a serving bowl and pour the "dressing" over, tossing to coat all. Add extra salt and pepper if desired.

Spicy Tomatoes and Green Beans

Sometimes you just need a pick-me-up and this dish will do it with the light flavor of cinnamon with tomatoes and green beans. Makes 6 servings.

What You'll Need:

4 cups of green beans (trimmed)
1 can of tomatoes (15 oz crushed)
1 1/4 cups of water
1/4 cup of onions (chopped)
3 tablespoons of olive oil
Salt and pepper
Cinnamon

How to Make It:

Add the 3 tablespoons to a skillet and sauté the 1/4 cup of onions. In a medium saucepan, add the 4 cups of green beans (trimmed), 1 can of tomatoes (15 oz crushed), 1 1/4 cups of water, sautéed onions, and dashes of salt and pepper and cinnamon. Stir and bring the water to a boil over high heat. Turn to medium low and simmer partial cover with a lid on for 35 minutes or until the green beans is tender. Season with more salt and pepper if desired.

Spinach Salad with Pomegranate Dressing

Spinach salad is a delicious meal made with pomegranate juice and walnuts, guaranteed to delight the taste buds. Makes 4 servings.

What You'll Need:

4 cups of spinach (baby)
1 cup of mushrooms (white button, sliced thin)
3/4 cup of tomatoes (grape, halved)
1/2 cup of walnuts (chopped)
1/4 cup of onions (thin sliced)
1/4 cup of pomegranate juice (plus 2 tablespoons)
1 tablespoon of apple cider vinegar
1 tablespoon of olive oil (extra virgin)
1 teaspoon of sugar (granulated)
Salt and pepper
Water and ice

How to Make It:

Pour 1/4 cup of pomegranate juice into a skillet and add the teaspoon of granulated sugar and a couple of dashes of salt. Turn heat to medium high and simmer for several minutes, stir often. Stir in the 1/2 cup of chopped walnuts and cook for another 5 minutes, the liquid should evaporate. Pour the nuts onto a cool baking sheet break apart when cooled.

Place the 1/4 cup of thin sliced onions in a bowl and cover with ice and water for 10 minutes. Drain the water and dry the onions with a paper towel. Put the 4 cups of baby spinach in a salad bowl, and then layer the cold onions, followed by the cup of thin sliced white button mushrooms, 3/4 cup of halved grape tomatoes, and the walnuts. In a separate bowl, combine the 2 tablespoons of pomegranate juice with the tablespoon of apple cider vinegar, tablespoon of extra virgin olive oil, and dashes of salt and pepper, using a whisk. Pour the dressing over the spinach salad and toss, and then serve.